Norfolk, VA
February 25, 1999
& geog regional

In 1998, the Norfolk Forum celebrates 65 years as the oldest non-profit, public speaking forum in the United States. This book has been published in honor of that celebration and as a testimony to the impact the Norfolk Forum, its board, members and subscribers have had on the cultural, social, and educational growth of the greater Hampton Roads community. The members and board of the Norfolk Forum wish to acknowledge our debt of gratitude to James E. "Gene" Justice, Forum board member, for his dedicated efforts in overseeing the chronicling of this rich history.

THE BEST TICKET IN TOWN

A History of
The Norfolk Forum

By Paul Chandler Moulton

HALLMARK
Publishing Company, Inc.

Congress shall make no law respecting an establishment of religion, or prohibiting the free exercise thereof; or abridging the freedom of speech, or of the press; or the right of the people peaceably to assemble, and to petition the Government for a redress of grievances.

—First Amendment, Bill of Rights

Hallmark Publishing, Inc.
Post Office Box 901
Gloucester Point, Virginia 23062

B.L. Walton, Jr., Owner and Publisher
Diana L. Bailey, Editor
Elizabeth B. Bobbitt and Robert B. Gilkeson, Graphic Designers
This volume has been edited according to the *Chicago Manual of Style,* 14th Edition, University of Chicago Press, 1993.

Library of Congress Cataloging in Publication Data

Moulton, Paul Chandler, 1959-
The best ticket in town: a history of the Norfolk Forum
by Paul Chandler Moulton
p.   cm.
Includes index.
ISBN 0-9653759-6-X   (alk. paper)
1. Norfolk Forum (Norfolk, Va.)—History.
2. Norfolk (Va.)—Intellectual life—20th century.
3. Lectures and lecturing—Virginia—Norfolk—History—20th century.
4. Norfolk (Va.)—History—20th century.
5. United States—Intellectual life—20th century.
6. United States—Politics and government—20th century.
I. Title.
II. Title: History of the Norfolk Forum.
F234.N8M68   1998
975.5'52104—dc21   98-43054
CIP

Printed in the United States of America

Table of Contents

Acknowledgments 7

Foreword by Dr. G. William Whitehurst 9

Chapter 1
The Creation 11

Chapter 2
The Founders 17

Chapter 3
The First Decade 27

Chapter 4
The Bomb, Cold War, and Civil Rights 45

Chapter 5
One Step Back, Two Steps Forward 63

Chapter 6
Return to Glory 75

Afterword
A Forward Look by William R. Van Buren, III 89

Appendix A
Norfolk Forum Speakers 90

Appendix B
Norfolk Forum Officers 95

Index 101

About the Author 104

The Center Theater served as the Forum's home from
the mid-1940s until 1972. Photograph courtesy of
Harrison Opera House.

Acknowledgments

This book has been written as a popular history and not as a scholarly work, therefore neither footnotes nor endnotes will appear. Where practical I have attempted to attribute the source of material within the narrative. However, that not always being practical, the following is a listing of where the documentary material used in the writing of this book can be located.

Quotes taken from letters to or from Lenoir Chambers are from the Lenoir Chambers Papers, #3827, Southern Historical Collection, Library of the University of North Carolina at Chapel Hill.

Quotes taken from letters to or from Louis I. Jaffé are from the Louis I. Jaffé Papers, #9924, Special Collections Department, University of Virginia Library.

P.N. Binford's letter to Mark A. McClaskey can be located at National Archives II, Record Group 215, Community War Services, Box 6, Regional Correspondence 1941-1942, Region IV, Norfolk, Virginia.

The report from the Committee for Congested Production Areas, Executive Office of the President, dated September 1, 1943, can be located at National Archives II, Record Group 207, Housing and Home Finance Agency, Box 7, File Norfolk, Va., Programs through 6/30/44.

The Norfolk Housing Authority resolution can be located in the Norfolk Housing Authority Minute Book I, 8/12/40 - 2/13/41, at the Norfolk Redevelopment and Housing Authority offices, Norfolk, Virginia.

Quotes attributed to lecturers or Forum officers, for the most part, have been taken from the *Virginian-Pilot*, and in a lesser degree from the *Ledger-Dispatch* and the *Ledger-Star*. An appendix at the end of this volume provides all known speakers and the date of their appearance before the Forum. This information should allow any future researchers to easily locate the source of the quote.

A very special thanks must go out to Jennifer Gregory Priest, senior archivist, Ohef Sholom Temple, for her assistance in locating information on Rabbi L.D. Mendoza; to Peggy Earle of the *Virginian-Pilot* who, as far as possible, provided copies of the *Pilot*'s subject index cards regarding the Norfolk Forum; and to Peggy A. Haile, the patient caretaker of the Sargeant Memorial Room, Norfolk Public Library.

My editor, Diana Bailey, has provided a sharp eye and a fine scalpel keeping my sometimes lengthy ramblings to a minimum, and has taught me some of the ins and outs of the publishing world.

As a former student of Dr. G. William Whitehurst, I am humbled and honored that Dr. Bill wrote such a wonderful foreword to this volume.

I wish to express my deepest and most sincere thanks to three people. I met Anthony and Celestine Dioguardi while the three of us were living in the tiny village of Thurso in Cathness County along the northwest coast of Scotland. I have been blessed to count them among my dearest friends for the last thirteen years. This book would not have been possible had they not opened their home to me, allowing me to write in peaceful solitude. Finally, I give my undying love and devotion to Deirdre S. Boyes whose constant encouragement and support, not to mention her keen mind, inspired me when the task at hand seemed too large. I thank each of you for your help and patience.

As always, Mr. Phelps, any errors are solely my responsibility.

Paul Chandler Moulton

FOREWORD

On looking back at the history of the Forum, I believe that I can claim to be among its pioneers. My early affiliation, however, was not as a paying member. It so happened that I was raised on Washington Park, one block from Blair Junior High School, in whose auditorium the first lectures were held. The decade of the 1930s, when the Forum was born, was the time of the Great Depression. A boy living in that era had to devise his own amusement, and I found mine in trying to gain admittance whenever there was an event at the Blair Auditorium, be it a play, a concert, or a lecture. Not having the price of admission, my standard tactic was to wait until the performance had begun, and with the attention of the ushers focused on the stage, I would creep in and try to find a spare seat.

Dr. G. William Whitehurst, long-time Norfolk resident and current professor at Old Dominion University, also briefly served as Norfolk Forum president before his election to the U.S. House of Representatives. Photograph courtesy of Dr. G. William Whitehurst.

My earliest recollection of a Forum lecture was in 1938 when, at the age of thirteen, I heard a lecture by a foreign correspondent recounting his experience in China, where conflict raged with Japanese invaders. Little did I realize then that one day I would sit on the stage as president of the Forum and introduce the speakers. If the memory of a young lad can attest to the interest of Forum speakers, it makes a statement about the quality of the programs, even then.

Throughout its long history, the Forum has consistently brought varied programs to the city, from political leaders to entertainers, but always of high quality. The fact that the Forum has been oversubscribed for so many years confirms the attraction of the programs. Nearly three generations of our area's citizens have enjoyed them, and although season ticket prices have risen over the years, it can still be said that the Forum is "the best ticket in town."

As the Forum approaches a new millennium, Hampton Roads can take pride that it initiated one of the most intellectually stimulating and entertaining enterprises in our community. The success of the past assures us that in the century to come the quality of the programs that has characterized them throughout the years will be the hallmark in the future.

DR. G. WILLIAM WHITEHURST

The mix of old and new is evident in this October 1934 photograph of City Hall Avenue. The Norfolk Forum began its second season this very same month. Photograph from the Isabella and Carroll Walker Collection; courtesy of Norfolk Public Library.

The quick reopening of the National Bank of Commerce on March 14, 1933, was an indication of Norfolk's generally sound economic situation. Photograph by Charles S. Borjes; courtesy of Norfolk Public Library.

Chapter 1
The Creation

Perhaps it was inevitable that the history of the Norfolk Forum would become steeped in legend. Tickets to the Forum, believed to be the oldest nonprofit, privately funded, public lecture series in the nation, are certainly difficult to obtain. Rumors have speculated that Forum tickets have been left to heirs in wills and even fought over in divorce settlements. Forum tickets are currently in such demand that there is a waiting list of several hundred prospective patrons anxious for their season ticket. It is also true that the Forum's lecturers have been legendary. Seven former heads of state and numerous Pulitzer Prize winners, including a Pulitzer Prize for Peace, and a Nobel Peace Prize recipient, all have graced the stages of the Norfolk Forum. An explanation of the Forum's mystique requires us to start at the beginning.

Since 1932 many explanations have circulated as to the founders and origins of the Norfolk Forum. *Virginian-Pilot* reporter Lucretia Libby McDine, writing in 1966, attributed the Forum's beginnings to an unknown businessman recently returned from a sojourn north where he was exposed to a lecture series. Speaking at a luncheon upon his return to Norfolk, he is said to have declared, "We don't have enough of that sort of thing in Norfolk. We should do something about it." William Ruehlmann, also writing for the *Pilot*, this time in 1983, attributed the creation of the Forum to "a bunch of school teacher[s]," who decided in 1933 that, "Norfolk could use a little intellectual shot in the arm." A 1954 editorial in the *Pilot* asserts, "the Forum was organized by a band of the undiscouraged in the depression days of 1932." Each of these explanations is, in part, both correct and incorrect.

What is indisputable is the fact that, for the last sixty-five years, the greater region of Hampton Roads, the city of Norfolk, and the Norfolk Forum have grown individually and as a community. The average Norfolkian separated by over a half century from the establishment of the Forum might find its survival rather remarkable. Born in defiance of the most pessimistic of times, the Forum not only survived, it also flourished. What follows is not only a history of the Norfolk Forum, its leaders and speakers, but also a history of a community.

As the tentacles of the Great Depression wrapped around all aspects of the American lifestyle, a small group of citizens in Norfolk, led by Dr. Vincent H. Ober, established a nonprofit public lecture series, the "Norfolk-Portsmouth Forum of Public Affairs." The mission of the new organization

was simple: to bring notable lecturers before the citizens of Norfolk. Organized in 1932, it shortened its name to the Norfolk Forum and presented its first series of lectures during the 1933-1934 social season. An understanding of the environment in which the Forum was established requires a quick look back to the years prior to the Forum's founding.

Given the national crisis of the Great Depression, one might well be skeptical of the survivability of a public speakers' forum. The reasons for the Forum's survival are varied, but at their core can be found the general soundness of Virginia's and Norfolk's economies, President Franklin D. Roosevelt's New Deal programs, and the devoted public service of the early founders.

On March 29, 1931, the *Virginian-Pilot* opined, "If there is any such thing as depression in Norfolk this spring it is not being felt in the Easter shopping which now is in full swing." According to Ronald L. Heinemann, in his monograph *Depression and the New Deal in Virginia*, between 1929 and 1940, Virginia experienced a commercial firm closing rate below the national average in all but two of those eleven years. This stability allowed Virginia's unemployment rate to remain below the national average. Norfolk's white unemployment rate in 1935 was an unbelievably low 2.5 percent. The African American unemployment figures, while higher than their white counterparts, stood at only 8 percent, a figure well below the national average. Of those Virginia citizens counted on the dole in the 1930 census, only 8.6 percent remained in that status by 1934. This percentage was the third lowest in the nation.

As with unemployment, bank closings in Virginia also remained below the national average. Norfolk experienced only one bank closing during the Great Depression, the African American-owned Metropolitan Bank and Trust in 1933. Rather astoundingly, by 1935, Virginians had regained 83 percent of their 1929 incomes, the fifth best rebound in the nation.

Norfolk benefited greatly from a number of federal projects. These New Deal construction programs accounted for the erection of Old Dominion University's Foreman Field, and aided in the completion of the Museum of Arts and Sciences building. Norfolk's African American population benefited from New Deal funding with the construction of the Norfolk Community Hospital, and African American women were also employed in the planting of the city's Azalea Garden. These programs, and others like them, ensured Norfolk experienced a steady influx of federal New Deal money.

The United States Navy, long tied to this seaport city, also contributed critical dollars to the area's economy. The Navy contracted for five destroyers and two battleships to be built in the Hampton Roads area in the late 1930s. Construction on a new naval hospital began in 1937, and the naval air station also increased in size.

While Virginia and Norfolk fared better than many sections of the country during the depression years, all was not bright. In 1932 Norfolk's city

Left: In this circa 1936 photo, a group of African American women receive instructions from a Works Project Administration supervisor prior to beginning work at what was to be called Azalea Garden and later Norfolk Botanical Garden, after it was combined with the adjacent Municipal Park. Photograph courtesy of Norfolk Public Library.

Right: WPA projects took many shapes. Pictured here are women in a 1936 sewing room project at Patrick Henry School. Photograph courtesy of Norfolk Public Library.

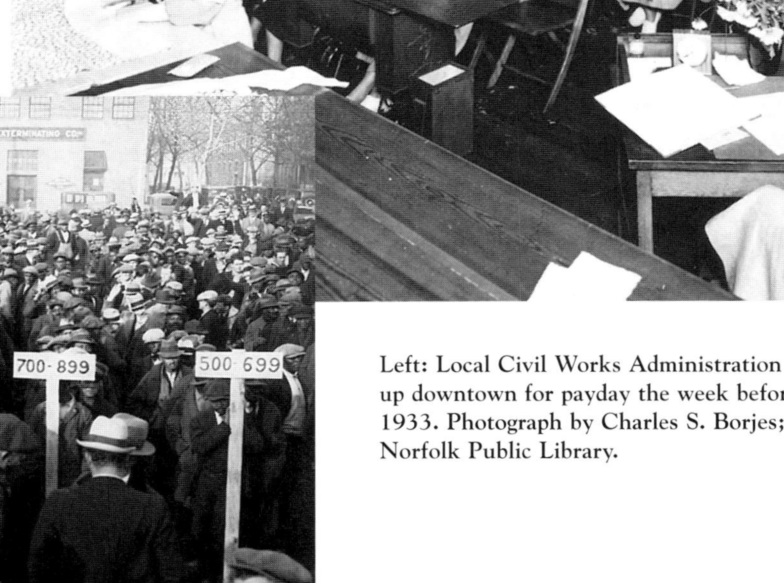

Left: Local Civil Works Administration workers queue up downtown for payday the week before Christmas, 1933. Photograph by Charles S. Borjes; courtesy of Norfolk Public Library.

council literally turned off the lights, extinguishing street lamps in an attempt to save $50,000. This action followed Norfolk's 10 percent pay reduction in the wages of its employees, and the dismissal of a number of police, fire, and garbage employees. In perhaps the worst year of the depression for Norfolk, the Ford Motor Company closed its plant during the last half of 1932 and early 1933. But, as Thomas C. Parramore, Tommy Bogger and Peter Stewart wrote in their book, *Norfolk: The First Four Centuries,* "for much of Norfolk's population, the Great Depression was little more than a temporary inconvenience," an inconvenience that Dr. Ober did not allow to hamper his efforts to establish a public lecture series in Norfolk.

Navy shipbuilding at local shipyards aided in lessening the effects of the Great Depression on the region's economy. The USS *Rowan* (DD405) and USS *Stack* (DD406) rest in Dry Dock No. 2, Norfolk Naval Shipyard, May 5, 1938, just before launching. U.S. Navy photograph.

The Hotel Monticello (left) hosted the meeting between Forum founders and the Foreign Policy Association's representative, William T. Stone, in 1932. The hotel, shown here circa 1938, also hosted many of the Forum's early speakers. Photograph by Carroll Walker; from the Isabella and Carroll Walker Collection; courtesy of Norfolk Public Library.

CHAPTER 2

THE FOUNDERS

Few documents remain extant from the Forum's early years, nonetheless there is some indication as to Dr. Ober's personal motivation in founding the Forum. One must bear in mind that these men and women were, for the most part, children of the New South, born and educated following the Civil War, who believed that the South, through industrialization and modernization, would far surpass in productivity and wealth not only other regions in the United States, but other countries as well. Paul M. Gatson, in his insightful study, *The New South Creed,* quotes Richard H. Emonds (in the *Manufacturers' Record,* 1889) in describing the New South leaders:

> It is the young men . . . who are making the South of today . . . They are filled with an enthusiasm that cannot be dampened. They are bold, earnest, energetic, and above all, they have a faith in the South's future that cannot be weakened.

Henry Steele Commager and Richard Brandon Morris, in their introduction to William E. Leuchtenburg's *Franklin D. Roosevelt and the New Deal,* wrote regarding Roosevelt's election that "Apathy, resignation, defeat, despair—these were foes that Roosevelt routed from the scene; action, advance, confidence, hope—these were the sentiments that he inspired in his followers. . . ." Certainly, as we shall see, the founders of the Forum, both men and women, were bold, earnest, energetic, confident, and hopeful of the future.

Born in Hudson Falls, New York, on July 11, 1899, Vincent H. Ober was the son of Merrill J. Ober. Merrill Ober later became a Norfolk educator and public school principal, serving as principal of the Prentis Park (Portsmouth), Henry Clay and James Monroe schools (both in Norfolk). He served as Monroe's principal for twenty years, from 1925 until his retirement in 1945. Merrill Ober was also instrumental in the establishment of Larchmont Methodist Church.

Vincent Ober attended public schools in Massachusetts and Portsmouth, Virginia, before attending the University of Virginia, University of Pennsylvania, and Temple University. He graduated from the Philadelphia College of Osteopathy in 1923. Following internships at Philadelphia

Osteopathic Hospital and Defur Hospital, Dr. Ober established a practice in Pitman, New Jersey, and remained there until his return to Norfolk in 1929.

Dr. Ober's interest in world affairs can be traced back to 1927 with a receipt acknowledging his five-dollar payment for a year's membership in the Philadelphia branch of the Foreign Policy Association [FPA]. This date is confirmed in the minutes of the May 16, 1991, Forum board of directors meeting. Dr. Ober, as special guest of Forum President Carter Grandy Scott for that meeting, "related that he had been a member of the [FPA] in Philadelphia in 1927." The FPA, through lectures and publications, worked to create an informed public opinion on issues of foreign policy confronting the nation. Based on available notes and records, it appears that Dr. Ober's association with the FPA extended into the early 1930s.

Believing Norfolk should have a similar association, Dr. Ober, in May 1932, headed a delegation of Norfolk citizens who met with William T. Stone at the Monticello Hotel in downtown Norfolk. A former newspaper writer, Stone joined the staff of the FPA in 1924 and became the director of the Washington, D.C., bureau in 1928. He served as a vice-president of the FPA from 1933 to 1941. It would seem that this explorative group met with Stone to discuss the creation of an FPA branch in Norfolk; however, that did not come to pass. The Forum's association with the FPA did not end there though. It would be renewed in January 1951, when Vera Micheles Dean, then director of the FPA's Research Department, spoke before the Forum calling for a constructive foreign policy that would wean the Russians from communism.

As can be seen in this early photograph, Forum founder Vincent Ober's vision was steady and determined. Photograph courtesy of V. Ober, Jr., son.

Perhaps uncertainty as to whether Norfolk could reach the FPA's minimum membership requirement of two hundred paid members discouraged the Norfolk group from forming an FPA chapter. The makeup of the Norfolk delegation—two attorneys, three clergymen, one newspaper editor, one naval officer, and two prominent Norfolk women—does show the broad background of the Forum's founders.

Stone may not have been able to convince the Norfolk delegation to form an FPA chapter, but his address obviously spurred Ober and the others to continue their pioneering work.

"The Norfolk-Portsmouth Forum of Public Affairs" came into existence shortly following the May 1932 conference with Stone. Dr. Ober served as the organization's first president with Alfred Anderson, local attorney, as vice-president, and Mrs. M.J. Caples, Norfolk School Board member, as the secretary-treasurer. According to a document donated to the Norfolk Forum by Dr. Ober shortly before his death in 1994, this group met in a variety of shapes and sizes throughout the fall, winter, and spring, planning the Forum's first season. In May 1933, the Forum publicly announced its plans for the coming season.

While it is clear that Dr. Ober's interest in public lectures began while he was a student in Philadelphia, it is also clear that his interest in public speaking did not end with the creation of the Forum. In 1935 the Kiwanis Club of Norfolk appointed Ober as the general chair of the club's Great Adventure Lecture Series. According to the October 3, 1935, issue of the *Virginian-Pilot*, children paid a nominal fee of twenty cents per lecture to help defray the cost of a two-week summer camp sponsored by the Kiwanis for underprivileged children. In 1934 and 1935 Ober served as the local chair of the annual gift drive for the Children's Home Society of Virginia. Not surprisingly, Ober began the 1934 local campaign with a lecture.

Dr. Ober's public service extended to many other social and professional societies as well. In the early 1940s Ober served as president of the Boys' Club of Norfolk. Ober also participated in the Rotary Club of Norfolk, the World Affairs Council of Hampton Roads, and the Virginia Osteopathic Association, which he led in the late 1930s. Ober's dedication in providing public service to his community is a trait shared throughout the Forum's early membership.

Dr. Vincent Ober was also a speaker himself, appearing on regular radio broadcasts for radio station WTAR. Photograph courtesy of Leroy Ober, brother.

Louis I. Jaffé, one of the Forum's co-founders and a former editor of the *Virginian-Pilot*, was born on February 22, 1888, in Detroit, Michigan. Jaffé relocated with his family to North Carolina in 1900 and, following his graduation from Trinity College (now Duke University), he worked as a reporter for the *Durham Sun*. In 1917, responding to the continuing conflict in Europe, Jaffé received a commission as a second lieutenant in the field artillery section, transferring in 1918 to the aviation section. Prior to his acceptance as editor of the *Virginian-Pilot* in 1919, Jaffé served with the Red Cross News Service in the Balkans. According to Alexander S. Leidholdt, in his book *Standing Before the Shouting Mob*, the years Jaffé spent in Europe during the war and during the immediate postwar period proved instrumental in "creat[ing] in [Jaffé] an acute and lifelong sensitivity to injustice."

Although a public figure, Jaffé was a very private individual. Leidholdt writes that Jaffé was a "[reluctant] participant in the civic and social activities expected of a newspaper editor, but he was reclusive and revealed himself best in his editorials." Jaffé, who did not like public speaking, claimed in a 1929 letter to William S. Meacham, future editor with the *Pilot*, that "there is surely no worse public speaker in the United States than myself." While Jaffé may have been a reluctant public figure he nonetheless served on several boards of directors, including Norfolk General Hospital,

Virginian-Pilot editor and Norfolk Forum co-founder Louis I. Jaffé (left) and *Virginian-Pilot* Associate Editor and future Forum President Lenoir Chambers both received the Pulitzer Prize for their editorial writing against racial injustice. Photograph courtesy of the *Virginian-Pilot*.

Norfolk Newspapers, Inc., and the Norfolk Council Committee on Higher Education.

As Leidholdt correctly asserts, Jaffé "revealed himself best in his editorials." Following an increase in racially motivated lynchings throughout the South in the mid-1920s, Jaffé wrote a series of editorials condemning Ku Klux Klan lynchings of African Americans. When other southern newspaper editors remained silent, Jaffé "directly and forcefully attacked the Klan" in his editorials, wrote Leidholdt. Through his editorials, Jaffé called on Governor Harry F. Byrd to introduce, and Virginia's General Assembly to enact, strong anti-lynching legislation. According to W. Fitzhugh Brundage, in *Lynching in the New South*, the legislation Byrd submitted to the Virginia General Assembly was drafted by Jaffé. On March 14, 1928, following approval by the General Assembly, Byrd signed the enacted legislation. The new statute, the state's first anti-lynching law, made any participant in a lynch mob an accessory to murder, and lynching itself a homicide.

Jaffé received the Pulitzer Prize for editorial writing in 1929 as a result of his anti-lynching editorials, the highest award ever bestowed upon a Virginia newspaper writer. Jaffé's interest in racial and social justice continued, and in the 1930s he was a member of the Virginia Commission on Interracial Cooperation.

This basic liberalism seems to have been present in many early members of the Forum. In a 1933 letter to Walter Lippman, *New York Herald Tribune* columnist, Jaffé wrote, "A large Norfolk group interested in public questions and prevailing liberal in their thinking, has organized a public forum," to discuss issues of the day. Jaffé then extended an invitation to Lippman to address the Forum in its inaugural season. Lippman, accepting no speaking engagements at the time, declined the Forum's invitation, becoming the first known speaker to reject an invitation from the Forum. Lippman was, however, on the schedule for the 1934-1935 season but canceled, becoming the second person, behind Dr. Robert E. Hutchens, to cancel a scheduled appearance before the Forum. (Existing records fail to indicate why they canceled.)

Dr. Louis D. Mendoza, rabbi of Ohef Sholom Temple and another principal founder of the Forum, typifies the liberal spirit Jaffé referred to in his letter to Lippman. Born in Cincinnati, Ohio, in September 1882, Mendoza graduated from the University of Cincinnati before attending Hebrew Union College where he received his rabbinical degree in 1906. After a brief stint as the director of the Sabbath School Extension of the Union of American Hebrew Congregations, Mendoza ascended to the rabbinate of the Ohef Sholom Temple in 1907 and remained at the Temple for the next thirty-eight years until his retirement in 1945. Thereafter, Dr. Mendoza served as rabbi emeritus until his death in 1954.

Though short in stature, Dr. Mendoza stood tall in the esteem of his fellow citizens. Winder R. Harris, managing editor of the *Pilot* and president of the Norfolk Forum, said of Dr. Mendoza upon his acceptance of the Golden Book Certificate in 1939 that Mendoza's "endow[ment of] a great heart and tolerant mind," had allowed him to "always [be] the courageous champion of the weak and underprivileged." (The Golden Book Certificate certifies that the recipient's name has been entered into the Golden Book of Jerusalem, one of the highest awards that can be bestowed upon a Jew.) In his acceptance speech Dr. Mendoza confirmed his work for tolerance and understanding by stating that he "will continue to introduce goodwill, replace ignorance with understanding, and banish prejudice" in his community.

In the mid-1930s, the Chamberlin Hotel, located on a federal reservation at Old Point Comfort, placed billboards throughout the area stating it catered to a Christian-only clientele. Having failed in his private efforts to have the offensive advertising altered, Dr. Mendoza wired his objections to Virginia senators Harry F. Byrd and Carter Glass, Secretary of the Navy Claude A. Swanson, and Secretary of War George Dern in October 1934. Mendoza wrote that the Christian-only advertising "by implication [is] one of the most offensive efforts that has been made to raise religious, race and social caste prejudices in America . . .. I do not take this action so much because my Jewish sensibilities are hurt as because I am an American citizen."

Dr. Louis Mendoza, Forum co-founder, strikes a reflective pose in this 1940s portrait. Photograph courtesy of Ohef Sholom Temple Archives.

A *Virginian-Pilot* editor agreed with Mendoza's charges of discrimination when he wrote that "the barring of Jewish people from the hotel constitutes discrimination against American citizens." Mendoza's telegram captured the attention of Byrd who, the *Pilot* reported on October 26, 1934, called upon Roosevelt "to use his influence to 'correct the condition.'" The previous day the *Pilot* reported that the Norfolk Advertising Board, a conservative organization headed by Francis E. Turin, had appealed "to the State Highway Commission to keep Virginia highways free of objectionable advertising." According to Jennifer Gregory Priest, senior archivist of Ohef Sholom Temple, the Chamberlin Hotel removed the objectionable billboards shortly thereafter.

Forum co-founder Governor Colgate W. Darden, Jr., (center) is pictured at a party November 25, 1941. Beside him are a Mr. Richardson (left) and a Mr. Story. Photograph by Charles S. Borjes; courtesy of Norfolk Public Library.

Dr. Mendoza's quest for understanding crossed denominational lines as well. In his memorial tribute, in the *1955 Central Conference of American Rabbis Yearbook*, Jacob Schwarz writes that Dr. Mendoza, as a "golden tongued orator" and a man of keen intellect, was welcomed to the pulpit of "every Christian church and on every lecture platform in the Norfolk area." Mendoza's interdenominational approach is best illustrated by the joint Thanksgiving service established between Ohef Sholom Temple and Freemason Street Baptist Church in 1927, a yearly service which has been celebrated now for seventy years.

Like Jaffé, Mendoza was also a private man. So too was their Forum co-founder Colgate W. Darden, Jr. Just like so many other young men his age, Darden served with the French Army in 1916, but when the United States entered the war in 1917, he came home to join the service, eventually rising to second lieutenant in the Marine Corps. Darden returned to Virginia after crippling injuries he sustained in an airplane crash. Unable to continue his military service, Darden gained his B.A. from the University of Virginia and his M.A. and LL.B. degrees from Columbia University prior to beginning studies at Oxford University.

Following Oxford, Darden joined the law practice of Virginia State Senator Jim Barron, the political leader of Norfolk. Shortly thereafter, Darden ran for a seat in the Virginia General Assembly's House of Delegates, serving two terms before standing for the U.S. House of Representatives. Elected in 1932, Darden served in the Seventy-third and Seventy-fourth Congresses. Upset in his 1936 reelection bid by Norman R. Hamilton (Forum board of directors, 1947), Darden returned to Norfolk and his law practice. Facing Hamilton again, this time as the challenger, Darden reclaimed his Second Congressional District seat in 1938, serving until his resignation in

1941. Darden resigned from Congress to undertake a bid for the governorship of Virginia, a position he held during the turbulent war years. Following his term as governor, Darden went on to become president of the University of Virginia, a position he held for twelve years.

Not only was Darden a founder and member of the Forum, but he also holds a unique position in its history. It appears that Darden was the only one-time Forum member to have formally addressed the organization. Darden spoke on January 20, 1954, in his capacity as president of the University of Virginia. His address focused on what he perceived as needed changes to the United Nations charter.

Given the times, one might assume that women in the 1930s held little or no social leadership roles in the community outside those they traditionally held, such as women's auxiliaries to fraternal organizations. In the case of the Norfolk Forum, that is simply not true. Women made significant and valuable contributions to both the Forum's formation and operation. And, like their male counterparts, they worked for understanding and tolerance. For example, Mrs. L.L. Newby, founding member of the "Norfolk-Portsmouth Public Affairs Forum" and a former president of the Woman's Club of Norfolk and the Virginia Federation of Woman's Clubs, attended a national conference for Christians and Jews in 1940 as the representative of the Woman's Club. Alice Jaffé, wife of Louis I. Jaffé, served a number of terms as a member of the Forum's board of directors and was also active in the Norfolk Woman's Council for Interracial Cooperation from 1945 until 1961. Mrs. Frederick Barrett, former Forum vice-president and board of directors member through the 1930s and 1940s, proved invaluable in the initial stages of membership recruitment for the Forum. But perhaps no other woman in the history of the Forum had as much input or influence as that of Miss Cherry Nottingham.

As chair of the Young Women's Christian Association's Public Affairs Committee in 1932, Nottingham became involved in the Forum's founding. Nottingham went on to serve the Forum in a variety of positions, including those of vice-president, secretary, and as a member of the board of directors until 1954. Beginning in 1955 and lasting until her death in 1965,

Forum members Thomas H. Willcox, first vice-president 1943-1948 (standing fourth from right), and Forum co-founder and dedicated Forum servant Miss Cherry Nottingham (seated second from right) are pictured in this group of lifelong friends during a 1959 social gathering. With them at the event are (standing, left to right) Jim Brooke, Mrs. Keville Glennan, Miss Mona Whittle, Mrs. Honoroa Mitchell Nottingham, Mrs. String, Willcox, Fanny Mayer, Alex Bell and Mary Carter Willcox; (seated left to right) Fanny Nottingham, Carrie Archer, Eloise Hunter, Hattie Hunter, Miss Nottingham, and Mrs. Jim Brooke. Photograph courtesy of Norfolk Public Library.

Nottingham held the ceremonial position of honorary vice-president of the Forum, a tribute to her long and dedicated service.

Louis I. Jaffé described Nottingham in a letter to John Steward Bryan, then president of the College of William and Mary, as "a woman of culture and refinement, traveled and at home in the modern world." The daughter of S. Severn Nottingham, one-time editor and publisher of the *Norfolk Landmark*, Nottingham studied at Barnard College (B.A.), Columbia University, the Sorbonne, the University of Madrid, and the University of Chicago (M.A.). Miss Nottingham devoted her life to the education of Norfolk's children—teaching French at Maury High School and later at the Norfolk Division of the College of William and Mary (now Old Dominion University)—and to the promotion of better understanding between the French and American cultures.

Her efforts in this latter field were recognized in 1933 by the French government when it bestowed upon her the *Palmes Academiques*. The award, subordinate only to the *Legion d'Honneur*, is given to individuals in the academy for outstanding achievement. The *Palmes Academiques* was not only given for Nottingham's work in promoting French culture in America, but also for her continuing work in "promoting charity toward all mankind."

While the *Palmes Academiques* was the highest award Nottingham received, it was not the last. In 1951 the American Association of University Women named a scholarship and an international fellowship in her honor. Four years later the Norfolk Business and Professional Woman's Club named Nottingham their Woman of Achievement in recognition of her lifelong work.

Apparent in the founders highlighted here is a deeply held belief in tolerance and understanding between peoples. However, these men and women operated within the structure of their society, a society that had two sides, one white and one black, segregated by social mores and codified law. Two former Forum members recall that the original bylaws called for the exclusion of African Americans. Since an extant copy of this document cannot be located, memories of the members cannot be independently confirmed. If the Forum had indeed opened its membership to the African American community of Norfolk, the public lectures would have been segregated in accordance with the Virginia Public Assemblage Act of 1926, commonly referred to as the Massenberg Act after its author George Alvin Massenberg of Hampton, Virginia. Considering the social structure of the times, it seems unlikely that the Forum, in its early years, was in a position to accept African Americans as members.

Given this brief examination of a few of the original founders of the Forum, we see a membership that is highly educated and slightly more progressive than the general community. This cross section of newspapermen, ministers, educators, and others, established the internal structure of the Forum and its practices. A public membership campaign began on June 5, 1933, with the establishment of an enrollment booth in the lobby of the Smith and Welton's department store. Requests for membership were also taken by J.E. Capps, president, Norfolk Forum, at his office in the Banker's Trust Building in Norfolk. This public membership drive began following an enthusiastic response to the proposed Forum at a spring garden party, hosted by Mrs. Frederick Barrett. During the garden party, various speakers involved in the development of the Forum explained the basic idea of the organization—to present to potential members a series of lectures from eminent individuals covering cultural, literary, and governmental issues before the nation. The *Pilot* reported on June 4, 1933, that this initial call for members resulted in roughly one hundred charter members.

The cost for a season's membership in the inaugural year was $1.00. This membership price remained in effect until the early 1940s when the price increased to $1.25 and, in 1945, to $1.50. A yearly membership entitled the ticket holder entrance to all four lectures and, like the Norfolk Community Concert Association, no tickets were to be made available for any single lecture. (This policy however, as we shall see, was not etched in stone.) The ability of the Forum's leadership to keep ticket prices down and continually present a slate of high quality speakers has earned the Forum a reputation, coined at some point in its long history, as "the best ticket in town."

The Forum's leadership determined that a minimum membership of 750 would be required to ensure a full slate of speakers, but Forum organizers aimed higher, setting their goal at 1,100 members. Following Mrs. Barrett's successful garden party, memberships sold quickly, and the Forum closed its membership rolls that first year with approximately 1,150 names inscribed, a result Forum President Capps reported "exceed[ed] all expectations." In what was to be a preview of times to come, the Forum, unable to fulfill all the ticket requests, returned several hundred membership requests that first year. This large demand for Forum tickets, coupled with the limited seating capacity of Norfolk's auditoriums, created a problem which has plagued Forum leaders ever since: a greater demand for seats than those available.

Unveiled at a garden party, the Forum was an idea that took at least a year and half to germinate and sprout. A fragile seedling planted in the dry dirt of the depression was cared for and watered by dedicated individuals from all walks of life. And when, in 1933, this perennial bloomed for the first time, Norfolk had something to be proud of, for that first season lived up to the high expectations of the Forum's leadership, featuring two major politicians, an authority on Asian affairs, and a newspaper editor. On October 29, 1933, Speaker of the House Henry T. Rainey (D-IL) opened what is now believed to be the longest running nonprofit, privately funded, public lecture series in the United States: the Norfolk Forum.

Blair Junior High School (pictured here shortly after its construction, circa 1923) was the Norfolk Forum's first home. Photograph courtesy of the Norfolk School Board.

Chapter 3
The First Decade

Between the Forum's first season and its tenth, the citizens of Norfolk witnessed a dramatically changing international, national, and local scene. Just as the clouds of the depression moved across the horizon in the late 1920s, war clouds had formed over Europe and Asia. Roosevelt, having led the country through the worst of the depression, broke George Washington's time-honored precedent by running for and winning a third term in 1940, and was contemplating an attempt at a fourth term. Roosevelt had also moved the country from a position of determined isolationism to arguably the preeminent world power and leader of the free world. These changes did not go unnoticed in Norfolk.

In the turbulent years of the Forum's first decade, Norfolk grew from a rather sleepy old southern seaport city to a rapidly growing urban center. Between 1940 and 1942, Norfolk's population increased by 25 percent, and by December 1943, the city's population had grown to 368,000. Unable to provide adequate housing and, at times, essential services to the influx of defense workers and military personnel, Norfolk ached with growing pains.

Few observers outside Norfolk had kind words for the city. In a letter from P.N. Binford, Field Recreation Representative, to Mark A. McClaskey, Director of Recreation for the Office of Defense Health and Welfare Services Region 4, Binford wrote, "To begin with Norfolk is not liked by visiting civilians any more than it is by servicemen." In March 1942, a *Collier's* magazine article characterized Norfolk as "a city out of control." Then early in 1943 the *American Mercury* called Norfolk the nation's "worst war town." The *Mercury's* article was not all negative, however. The author noted that "Norfolk seemed to have a progressive, honest city government, functioning as efficiently as it can under" adverse conditions.

This displeasure does not seem to have applied to visitors sponsored by the Norfolk Forum. A letter written by John Goette gives a distinctly different impression. Goette wrote to Forum President Lenoir Chambers on October 29, 1943, of his "extremely nice memories of Norfolk," and that "Nothing could have been more inspiring than seeing the Naval Base and talking with your friends."

The Forum too saw changes. Like the city itself, the Forum's first decade was marked by growth, a little controversy, and a lot of diversity. Just as city leaders functioned as efficiently as possible, so too did the Forum's leaders. Under the direction of J.E. Capps, Winder Harris, and Lenoir Chambers, the Forum had a remarkable first decade.

The early years of the Forum saw amazing continuity in the Forum's officers. J.E. Capps, an insurance agent for Pacific Mutual Life Insurance Company, served as president of the Norfolk Forum from 1933 until his resignation in June 1938. Capps, who in 1937 lead all Pacific Mutual agents in sales, received his B.A. from the College of William and Mary and his M.A. from Columbia University. In announcing Capps' position as the company's top agent, Pacific Mutual praised him as an "esteemed . . . citizen of the first rank," and "a leader of true championship caliber," traits that Capps applied to his leadership of the Forum. While the reasons for Capps' resignation as the Forum's president in 1938 are unknown, it might have resulted from the travel his new position as president of the Big Tree Club required. (The Big Tree Club was an organization of company agents who sold over $200,000 in life insurance.)

In 1933 and 1934 Capps was aided by Edward Stanley Brinkley (first vice-president), Mrs. Frederick R. Barrett (second vice-president), Mrs. W.L. Harrell (recording secretary), Cherry Nottingham (corresponding secretary), and Roy W. Dudley (treasurer). Winder R. Harris served as the chair of the Program Committee from 1933 until assuming the presidency in June 1938. This group, and those who followed, led the Forum through a period of rapid growth and a just-as-rapid constriction.

The Forum's membership was limited to the 1,000 or so seats available in the auditorium of Blair Junior High School. It was in this auditorium that the Forum presented the majority of their lectures between 1933 and 1947. Even with this limited seating the Forum, under Capps, increased its membership from 1,150 to 1,350 for the 1934-1935 season. With a year's experience, the Forum's leadership realized that not every member attended each lecture, therefore more tickets could be sold than actual seating would permit. The Forum's leadership also made tickets available to single lectures at the door at a cost of $1.00, or the amount of a season's subscription. The

The Forum's second treasurer, Roy Dudley (standing) is pictured on January 22, 1948, with Oscar Smith upon the latter's acceptance of Norfolk's First Citizen Award for 1947. Also pictured are Mrs. Roy Dudley (left) and Mrs. Oscar Smith. Photograph by Charles S. Borjes; courtesy of Norfolk Public Library.

number of tickets available on the night of a lecture was limited to the number of empty seats remaining following the seating of all Forum members. This practice has continued off and on throughout the Forum's history.

Season subscriptions were a matter of faith in the early years of the Forum. Unlike today when the following season's speakers are announced in April or May, the announcement of speakers during the early years often did not occur until September or October, even though the membership drives were held in May. The Forum did, on occasion, list prospective speakers in membership drive announcements as an indication of whom the Forum was pursuing for the upcoming season.

As in the first year, tickets for the second season sold quickly. By the time the public membership drive began on May 1, 1934, 725 charter members had renewed their subscriptions, leaving a mere 625 subscriptions for public consumption. The *Pilot* reported approximately 125 people joined the Forum on the first day of the public membership drive, which once again had a headquarters booth at Smith and Welton's. The setup of this booth appears to have occurred only during the first two years of the Forum, for there is no mention of it in subsequent news reports. With an already dedicated following, the Forum may have found it easier for prospective members to mail their requests to Capps at his office in the Banker's Trust Building.

This phenomenal demand for tickets continued into the 1935-1936 season. By March 1935, Forum officers had received 1,650 applications for the upcoming lecture season. On June 9, 1935, the *Pilot* reported that requests for Forum memberships had exceed the seating capacity of any theater in Norfolk. The Forum, faced with an overwhelming demand for tickets and still limited to the seating capacity of Blair Auditorium, explored the possibility of relocating the Forum to another venue.

The Forum's leadership negotiated with both the Colonial Theater and the City Auditorium in a failed attempt to move the Forum out of Blair. It is not clear why the Colonial Theater was rejected. The theater was available under binding contract and had acceptable acoustics. The Forum, always operating with just enough overhead to get by, may have found the fee for the Colonial Theater beyond its means. As late as 1945, the Forum paid only $12.50 to the Norfolk School Board for each use of Blair Auditorium with an additional $3.50 for janitorial services. The City Auditorium, on the other hand, was not available under binding contract, allowing it to be booked for other events. In addition, the City Auditorium was deemed unusable at the time because of its poor acoustics. Neither of these hindrances, however, would block its later use.

J.E. Capps, as president of the Norfolk Forum, was acutely aware of Norfolk's need for a large auditorium worthy of hosting lectures as well as musical presentations. Norfolk City Manager Thomas P. Thompson appointed Capps as chair of an advisory committee in February 1935 to explore the possibility of obtaining federal Public Works Administration funding to build an auditorium for the city. Previously, in 1922, the city had also explored the possibility of building a venue that would seat 7,500 at a cost of $750,000.

This proposal, however, came to naught, and the city remained without a first class auditorium. The city did, however, open the federally funded Municipal Auditorium in 1943, allowing the United Service Organization (USO) to operate the facility for the duration of the war.

Having rejected moving the series to another location, the Forum's executive board made a drastic two-part decision. First, the Forum increased its membership limit from 1,350 to 1,900. Even this increase proved inadequate, with an estimated 2,500 members attempting to subscribe for the 1935-1936 season. Second, the executive board decided to present each speaker for two consecutive nights in Blair Auditorium.

This arrangement required some interesting attendance arrangements. Color-coded

The Norfolk Forum was not the only organization to present high profile speakers to the citizens of Norfolk. Here journalist H.V. Kaltenborn (center) arrives for a lecture at Blair Auditorium on September 21, 1943. Norfolk Mayor Joseph Wood is to the left of Kaltenborn. The sponsor for this event is not known. Photograph by Charles S. Borjes; courtesy of Norfolk Public Library.

tickets were issued to members, indicating which lecture they were to attend. For example, in announcing playwright Cosmo Hamilton's appearances on October 19-20, 1936, the *Pilot* informed Forum members that "holders of orange tickets may hear tomorrow night's lecture. Those holding green tickets will attend Tuesday night." Further, if a member attended the first night of the first lecture, he or she would then attend the second night of the second lecture. The membership continued to alternate first night, second night for the remaining two lectures. The Forum made every attempt to honor requests for same-night seating from groups who wished to attend the lectures together.

This two-night arrangement continued, for the most part, throughout the 1936-1937 season, although two of the five lectures presented that season were held at the City Auditorium for a single night only. Senator Alben William Barkley addressed the first Forum meeting held in the City Auditorium on January 18, 1937. Barkley, who later served as Harry S Truman's vice-president from 1949 to 1953, addressed an estimated 2,000 Forum members regarding, "Present Day Social And Economic Problems." The second lecture held at the City Auditorium did not draw as large an audience. George Fort Milton, editor of the *Chattanooga News*, speaking on Pan-Americanism, drew only 700 members due in part to inclement weather. With psychologist Dr. Lewis Berg's lecture, the Forum returned, for one lecture, to Blair Auditorium.

The 1937-1938 season saw the Forum return to the City Auditorium, with lectures being held for only one night. This move to the auditorium was intended to be a permanent shift. Capps, explaining the move in the March 17, 1937, *Pilot*, stated that, with the increased seating of the City Auditorium, the Forum could accommodate all of its members, estimated then at 2,000. This decrease of 500 from the 1935-1936 season might have resulted from the somewhat complex attendance schedule. Furthermore, lectures were again held for only one night. Capps explained that this reduction in overhead increased funds available for speakers, ensuring the Forum's continued success in presenting programs of the highest caliber.

The relationship between the city's larger auditoriums and the Norfolk Forum proved to be a rocky one. For scme reason, the Forum's 1938-1939 season returned, once again, to Blair Auditorium, with membership limited to the one-night seating capacity of Blair. The Forum continued to hold its lectures at Blair through the 1942-1943 season. But, for the 1943-1944 season, the Forum moved into the newly built USO Auditorium. The USO organization required the Forum to limit its membership to 1,300 and distribute the remaining tickets to servicemen and women free of charge. The inability of Forum leaders and the USO to come to an understanding beneficial to them both regarding use of the auditorium resulted in the Forum moving back, once again, to Blair Junior High School with the final lecture of the 1943-1944 season. The Forum would continue to hold its lectures at Blair Auditorium until October 13, 1947, when Rear Admiral E.M. Zacharias, a United States Navy intelligence officer, addressed the Forum in the Center Theater.

The Forum not only faced internal problems as a result of its rapid growth but also outside competition. On October 28, 1938, the *Ledger-Dispatch* reported that a new lecture organization, the Norfolk Town Meetings, was being organized. Under the direction of Dr. Ernest W. Gray with the assistance of Forum co-founders, Rev. C.M. Gordon, Rabbi L.D. Mendoza, and Cherry Nottingham, the

Senator Robert M. La Follette, Jr., and Representative Hamilton Fish, Jr., pose with Forum members at a welcoming ceremony. Pictured are (left to right): J. Carlton Hudson, La Follette, Forum President J.E. Capps, Fish, and Charles T. Abeles, future Forum president. Photograph courtesy of Norfolk Public Library.

Norfolk Town Meetings' internal organization was modeled after the Norfolk Forum. The Town Meetings would be held on a nonprofit basis with a question-and-answer period at the end of each lecture. Dr. Gray pointed directly at the Norfolk Forum when he explained, in the *Virginian-Pilot*, why the Town Meetings were begun:

> The fact that half of those who applied for membership in
> the Norfolk Forum were refused because of a lack of accom-

modations indicates that there is a keen interest in critical problems today and a real need for another organization to bring to our city the best in American thought on problem topics of national and world concern.

Winder R. Harris served as managing editor of the *Virginian-Pilot* from 1921 until his election to Congress from Norfolk's Second Congressional District in 1941. He was president of the Norfolk Forum from 1938 to 1941. Photograph courtesy of the *Virginian-Pilot*.

The Forum's estimated 2,000 members for its 1937-1938 season shows why Dr. Gray believed the city could support two lecture series.

Other Norfolk-based organizations also provided national speakers as part of their regular programs. The Rotary Club of Norfolk began featuring speakers of renown at its luncheons in 1914. The Executive Club in 1939 began presenting speakers at the club's private luncheons. Also, in 1939 the Norfolk Division of the College of William and Mary began presenting local professors during a regular lecture program. As early as 1935, the Irene Leache Memorial presented a wide variety of lecturers to the Norfolk public.

Portsmouth also developed its own speakers program. The *Virginian-Pilot* reported on May 11, 1939, that the Portsmouth Forum's membership drive would close at the beginning of the following week. The Portsmouth Forum sought the same high quality speakers as did the Norfolk Forum, including Dr. Will Durant, Ruth Bryan Owen, and Robert M. La Follette, Jr. The Norfolk Forum would continue to face competition throughout its existence.

Winder R. Harris, president from 1938 to 1941, continued the growing tradition of local newspaper editors and future politicians providing leadership in the Forum. Harris, described by Lenoir Chambers in *Saltwater & Printer's Ink* as a "powerfully built" man with a forceful personality who possessed "gifts as a conversationalist and public speaker," was born in Wake County, North Carolina, on December 3, 1888. Harris started his newspaper career with the *Raleigh Times* in 1908. During the 1920 presidential campaign, Harris, working for the Universal News Service, traveled with democratic presidential nominee James M. Cox. Harris then followed the Progressive Party's nominee for president, Robert M. La Follette, Jr., in 1924. From 1925 until his nomination for

Samuel Northern (second from right), Forum treasurer from 1938 until 1943, is seen with (left to right) Charles Kaufman, Daniel Thornton, and E.T. Gresham. The individual on the far right is unidentified. Photograph by Carroll Walker; from the Isabella and Carroll Walker Collection; courtesy of Norfolk Public Library.

Congress in 1941, Harris served as the managing editor of the *Virginian-Pilot*. Like Colgate W. Darden, Jr., before him, Harris was elected to Congress from Virginia's Second Congressional District, serving until his resignation on September 16, 1944.

Harris' public service was not limited to politics. He served as president of the Norfolk Forum, Rotary Club of Norfolk and the Norfolk Community Fund. For eleven years, Harris hosted a local radio show sponsored by the National Bank of Commerce, called "High Spots of the Week's News." Harris' involvement with the broadcast ended with his resignation from Congress. The Cosmopolitan Club of Norfolk recognized Harris for his dedicated public service by presenting him with the club's coveted Distinguished Service Award for 1934. His contributions to the Norfolk Forum did not go unnoticed either. In May 1941, following Harris' defeat of fellow Forum member Norman R. Hamilton in the Second Congressional District race, Harris was made the Forum's honorary president. This was the first of four times in the Forum's history that a member would be so honored. (The others were Charles T. Abeles, honorary president, 1950-1951; Cherry Nottingham, honorary vice-president, 1955-1965; and Dr. Vincent H. Ober, honorary director, 1992-1994.)

Under Harris' leadership, the Forum began to explore the possibility of incorporating. On June 2, 1941, incorporation papers were signed by Whit P. Tunstall, president; Michael B. Wagenheim, second vice-president; and

Besides Rabbi Mendoza, other members of the Ohef Sholom Temple were active leaders of the Norfolk Forum. Long-time officer and board member (1930s-1950s) Michael Wagenheim (seated right) and Alan J. Hofheimer (standing, second from right) are pictured here, circa 1972, with other members of the temple, including (standing, left to right) William Oberndorfer, (unknown), Lester Sherrick, Harry Mansbach, Ralph Margulis, Hofheimer, and Mike Lazaron; (seated, left to right) Harry Kanter, Charles Kaufman, and Wagenheim. Photograph by Carroll Walker; from the Isabella and Carroll Walker Collection; courtesy of Norfolk Public Library.

The Norfolk Newspaper Building, new headquarters for the *Virginian-Pilot*, was dedicated October 28, 1937, the date this photograph was taken. Many of the city's newspaper editors were leaders of the Norfolk Forum. Photograph by Carroll Walker; from the Isabella and Carroll Walker Collection; courtesy of Norfolk Public Library.

Samuel T. Northern, treasurer. The Forum's purpose, as stipulated in the certificate of incorporation, was "the promotion of learning and literary merit among its members; to conduct a public forum on matters of general interest . . .[and] simply to stimulate and promote the moral, social and educational welfare of its members."

Following the two-year term of Whit P. Tunstall as Forum president, Lenoir Chambers began his term in 1943. Born in Charlotte, North Carolina, on December 26, 1891, Chambers was, according to Alexander S. Leidholdt in *Standing Before the Shouting Mob*, "removed from the masses by birth, education and position." His high school education at Woodberry Forest School in Orange, Virginia, is an indication of his upbringing.

Following his graduation from the University of North Carolina in 1914, Chambers returned to Woodberry to teach for two years prior to joining the junior class at the journalism school of Columbia University. Fellow Columbia students and Chambers attempted to gain the World War I government information work that eventually went to George Creel and the Committee on Public Information. Failing in this endeavor, Chambers joined the 52nd Infantry of the Sixth Division, United States Army, following his officer's training in Tennessee.

After the war, and following positions with the University of North Carolina News Service and the *Greensboro Daily News*, Chambers joined the *Virginian-Pilot* in 1929 as an associate editor under Louis I. Jaffé. When the editorial-ship of the *Ledger-Dispatch* became available, Chambers was transferred by the newspaper's parent company to the *Ledger-Dispatch*. Chambers remained with the *Ledger-Dispatch* until Jaffé's death in 1950, when he assumed editorial leadership of the *Pilot*.

Three-term Norfolk Forum President Lenoir Chambers (right) is pictured with *Saltwater & Printer's Ink* co-author Joseph Shanks in 1967. Photograph by Max Hertweck; courtesy of Norfolk Public Library.

Chambers, like Jaffé, did not like public speaking. Leidholdt asserts that Chambers "abhorred public speaking and did his best to engage in it as seldom as possible." It must have been difficult for the editor, as a member of the prestigious German Club, Norfolk Yacht and Country Club and the Virginia Club, not to mention his duties with the Norfolk Forum, to avoid public speaking. The Lenoir Chambers Papers (part of the Southern History Collection at the University of North Carolina) and newspaper accounts reveal that Chambers introduced at least seven Forum speakers between 1939 and 1952. Interestingly, Chambers assumed the duties of Harris' weekly radio address upon Harris' departure from the broadcast. For someone not fond of public speaking, this position seemed an unlikely vocation for Chambers.

In his introduction of Herbert Agar, associate editor of the *Louisville Courier-Journal*, to the Forum's audience on November 8, 1939, Chambers described a new breed of southern newspaper editors. Chambers' description not only illuminated those new editors, but also, in a way, the membership of the Forum:

> Instead of being, for the most part, provincial and sectional, they are national and cosmopolitan. Instead of being bound by their surroundings, they are citizens of the world . . . they are helping to revolutionize Southern thinking, to a better understanding of our times, and perhaps even of the future.

Cars jam Granby Street following the end of gas rationing on August 16, 1945. In spite of rationing, Forum events still filled the audience. Photograph by Charles S. Borjes; courtesy of Norfolk Public Library.

Clearly, this description fits the purpose of the Forum as outlined in the 1941 certificate of incorporation. Chambers' belief in this aspiring idealism among southern newspaper editors, and by extension the purpose of the Norfolk Forum, would be severely tested in the final years of the 1950s.

Under Chambers, the Forum discarded the more formal dinner attire. In letters to economist Beardsley Ruml in October 1944 and January 1945, Chambers stressed that during the war it "is our custom . . . for the speaker and the chairman of the meeting to wear business clothes." Again in November 1945, in a note to Max Hill upon his arrival in Norfolk (a courtesy extended by Chambers to each speaker during his presidency), Chambers reminded him "that our speakers are wearing business clothes, not dinner coats, this year." The war years do not appear to be the only time the Forum abandoned its black-tie requirement of the speaker. As late as February 25, 1954, Chambers, in a welcoming letter to Edward A. Weeks, refers to some confusion in what Weeks is expected to wear. "Mr. Wagenheim [first vice-president] and I have been uncertain on the matter of clothes . . .. Frequently the Forum speakers wear dinner coats, but there is no requirement . . .. We should like [you] to wear what you wish."

The Forum also faced, under Chambers' administration, the prohibition of private pleasure driving during the war years. Beginning on January 7, 1943, the Office of Price Administration banned pleasure driving to save vital fuel for the war effort. Civic and social functions planned for that evening were canceled throughout Norfolk. However, the Forum, not deterred by the Great Depression, also would not be deterred by this latest inconvenience. The program with journalist Hallett Abend went on as scheduled. The *Virginian-Pilot* estimated attendance at 600 members, a drop of 400 from the Forum's average attendance. The *Pilot* also reported that only six cars were parked outside Blair Junior High School on the night of the lecture.

Neither Chambers nor Forum Secretary Cherry Nottingham desired to serve a third term in 1945. Nottingham, writing to Chambers on May 5, 1945, informed Chambers that it had "been a great pleasure to serve the Forum, and you yourself, as President, and I shall always remember my tenure of office as a real privilege." Nottingham's resignation may have been in response to Chambers announcing his own resignation. Two days prior to Nottingham's resignation, Chambers wrote to the board of directors he would be unable to "continue another year as president."

Chambers' decision brought an immediate response from fellow board members. William Herbert Nash, Forum director, replied to Chambers on May 5, 1945, that Chambers was the best "qualified for the position as President of the Forum than most anyone I know, and I do not believe that we should attempt to ride a free horse to death, but I do hope that you will reconsider." Martha R. Montague, also a member of the Forum's board of directors, writing on the fifth of May, expressed her regret to Chambers that she would be unable to attend the upcoming board meeting "to join with the others in encouraging you [Chambers] to reconsider your decision to resign."

The pressure on Chambers to remain as president was too great for him to resist. Nottingham expressed her delight that Chambers had "consented to guide the destinies of the Forum this year," in a letter to Chambers on May 22, 1945. With Chambers returning to the Forum's presidency for another year, Nottingham also returned, serving as secretary for the 1945-1946 and 1946-1947 seasons.

There has been, as seen in the first chapter, a number of explanations as to why the Forum was formed. One explanation not previously mentioned holds that the Forum was organized to keep track of the ever-changing New Deal programs of President Roosevelt. This belief may have come about because of the Forum's selection of House Speaker Henry T. Rainey as its first lecturer. Rainey's lecture, entitled "Better Days Ahead, America," covered steps taken by the Roosevelt administration to end the depression. Rainey went so far as to credit the New Deal with driving communism from the shores of the United States. Roosevelt's opponents, however, would certainly argue that the New Deal did more to bring socialism to America's shores than any other event or programs in the ideology's short history.

An examination of the speakers who addressed the Forum and their topics that first year, however, shows a diversity in experiences and beliefs not limited to New Deal issues. House Speaker Rainey was followed by the writer Upton Close who spoke on events in Asia. Close likened Japanese imperialism to a sword pointed at the United States, and warned Americans "to divest themselves of indifference and foolish optimism and face squarely the threat from the Orient." The Forum's third lecturer, Max Forrester Eastman, was the former editor of the radical political and literary journal *The Masses*, a publication considered so dangerous by the federal government that its editors were arrested and tried twice in 1918 for their opposition to the United States' involvement in World War I. Eastman, a one-time supporter of the

Soviet Union, had in recent years grown increasingly disenchanted with Soviet leadership and had written several books, including his 1934 publication of *Artists in Uniform*, a penetrating study of Communism in practice that attacked developments within the Soviet Union. While unverified, it would seem logical that his talk that evening warned against the then-fashionable admiration of the Soviet Union.

The season concluded with former United States Senator Henry J. Allen addressing conditions in Europe and Asia. Speaking in March 1934, Allen predicted that war would break out between the Soviet Union and Japan within a few months and that the rest of Europe would be at war within three to four years. Allen may have feared a war between Japan and the Soviet Union was imminent as a result of Roosevelt's official recognition of the Soviet Union in November 1933. This put Japan, as Walter Lafeber in the *American Age* phrased it, between the arms of the nutcracker.

A further examination of the Forum's lecturers during that first decade gives additional insight into the speakers. Journalists were the predominant choice of the program committee, followed by educators, members of Congress, other high-ranking government officials—including statesmen, ambassadors, and a former head of state—three previous or future Pulitzer Prize recipients, and finally a local-boy-turned-Rhodes Scholar, Stringfellow Barr.

The topics were just as varied and wide ranging as the men and women invited to address the Forum. As uneasiness grew in Europe and Asia, the interest of the Forum's membership shifted to those areas of the world. Therefore, not surprisingly, conditions in Asia and Europe dominated the topics speakers chose. But the economic problems of the world were not forgotten. The Forum's first debate between Progressive Senator Robert M. La Follette, Jr., and Republican Representative Hamilton Fish dealt with the success or failure of the New Deal. Other topics included international economics, current social and cultural problems, birth control, entertainment, international diplomacy, and two lectures regarding Pan-Americanism.

Perhaps the speaker who best demonstrates the variety of the Forum's interest was philosopher, author and Pulitzer Prize winner Will Durant. Durant was the only individual to address the Forum membership twice in the 1930s and a record of four times between 1935 and 1957. The frequency of his appearances is especially noteworthy considering that he went into seclusion in 1935 to research and write.

Durant, in his first lecture before the Forum on March 14, 1935, touched on three major topics. First and foremost, Durant advocated increasing the use of birth control for those he deemed "the great majority of people who do not have ability," to decrease the number of children this group generated. His corollary then, was that those "most intelligent and capable of our people" must reduce their use of birth control in order to produce the leaders of the future. Secondly, Durant predicted that Japan, as a result of its own economic distress, might declare war over China. Finally, Durant decried the loss of unity within the United States as a result of increased immigration.

On his second visit to the Forum, Durant returned to his Japanese theme. On January 6, 1938, Durant, whose lecture was entitled "The World Conflict—Communism, Fascism and Democracy," told an audience of over 2,000 that Europe must unite to "control Japan . . .. I am interested in preserving Western Civilization. Therefore, I beg of you, don't hate Italy. Don't hate Germany." Durant called on Great Britain to make concessions to Italy and Germany, thereby freeing the British fleet from duties in the Mediterranean Sea. Once freed, the king's fleet could join with forces from France and the United States to confront Japan.

Durant's perspective of the Far East softened slightly over time. In his 1951 address to the Forum, he promoted a closer alliance with the Orient, but his basic disbelief in the equality of people does not appear to have changed. In his 1957 address to the Forum, he argued that elimination of the weak and the survival of the strongest was a historical fact. Therefore, there could be no human equality. In his own words, "A Utopia based on hope of human equality is a dream . . . inequality may be unfortunate but it's natural."

The first debate held by the Forum, as already mentioned, was between Senator Robert M. La Follette, Jr., and Representative Hamilton Fish on March 26, 1938. La Follette advocated that the central government should aid in the growth of a nation's wealth. As might be expected, Fish proposed a reduction in both taxes and government-imposed business regulations. The result, Fish argued, would be a "restore[d] business confidence." Each gentleman was allowed to make an opening statement and then, as usual, the floor was opened for questions.

The question-and-answer period following the lecturer's formal presentation has proved to be one of the more enduring aspects of the Forum. Following his appearance before the Forum September 12, 1944, Ray Josephs, author of *Argentine Diary*, sent a thank-you letter to Chambers in December 1944. Josephs wrote, "I do feel your group was one of the most stimulating and interested of all those I have addressed on my present tour—and the questions certainly proved their interest." Seventeen months later Josephs, preparing for a trip to Latin America, again wrote to Chambers. Josephs recalled the "interest down in Norfolk" regarding Latin America and requested Chambers inform him as to possible "questions likely to be on the minds of people regarding Latin America." There appears to be little doubt that the insightfulness of Forum members had a lasting effect on Josephs.

The debate format must have been considered a success, since the 1938-1939 season began with a debate. Before 1,000 Forum members, Dr. No-yung Park, a native of Manchuria, and Dr. Yutaka Minakuchi, a native of Japan, discussed current Sino-Japanese relations. Japan had moved into and occupied Manchuria during the years 1931-1932 and established a puppet government to oversee their new 400,000-square-mile territory. In 1936 Chinese Leader Chiang Kai-shek declared war on Japan, which resulted in a full-scale attack by the Japanese against China in 1937. Both Park and Minakuchi agreed, in what the *Pilot* termed a good-natured debate with sharp charges and explanations, that the current war could continue for ten years, a prediction that proved very close to being correct.

Stringfellow Barr, born in Suffolk, Virginia, in 1897, and a former Norfolk resident, spoke to the Forum on March 8, 1940. Barr had attended Norfolk schools in his early years and graduated from the University of Virginia in 1917 with an M.A. degree. From 1919 to 1921 he was a Rhodes Scholar at Oxford University. Barr was well known in Norfolk and, after his return to the United States, he frequently visited relatives living in Norfolk. During the late 1920s Barr provided editorials to the *Pilot* when the paper's regular editorial writers were on holiday or when an emergency arose. Elected president of St. John's College in 1937, and in cooperation with the University of Chicago, Barr was conducting an experiment in liberal education. This experiment required students to read and understand the "great books," vice normal academic studies.

During the early years of the Norfolk Forum a membership card took the place of individual tickets. Pictured here is Forum member T.D. Savage's 1941-1942 membership card. There are two items of interest to note about the 1941-1942 season. First is foreign affairs expert Henry C. Wolfe's lecture five days prior to Pearl Harbor, and Dr. Ricardo Alfaro was the first former head of state to address the Norfolk Forum. Membership card courtesy of Toy D. Savage, Jr.

NORFOLK FORUM, Incorporated
Program for the Season 1941-42

Blair Auditorium 8:15 P. M.

Anne O'Hare McCormick .... Saturday, Nov. 8, 1941
Henry C. Wolfe .... Tuesday, Dec. 2, 1941
Dr. Ricardo Alfaro .... Friday, Jan. 9, 1942
Edwin Hartrich .... Wednesday, Feb. 11, 1942

No..........................

The first woman to address the Forum was Ruth Bryan Owen, ambassador to Denmark, on November 27, 1934. The daughter of William Jennings Bryan and a former congresswoman, Owen became the first woman diplomat in the United States Foreign Service when she was appointed as the Minister Plenipotentiary and Envoy Extraordinary to Denmark. In keeping with the Forum's practice of having speakers wear dinner attire, the *Pilot* reported that Owen wore a "dress of black lace, with a corsage of purple orchids supplying the only touch of color."

Owen focused on the Danes' perception of Americans during her lecture. The Danes, she said, saw America as an odd land filled with crime, frog racing, tree-sitting, marathon dancing, and pie-eating contests. She attributed this perception to Danish news coverage that focused on crime in the United States, and to the motion picture industry for creating an unreal image of America. Regarding the Danes, Owen praised their almost "idyllically simple" rural lifestyle along with "their honesty, frugality, industry and hospitality."

The Forum brought its first former head of state before its audience in 1942. Dr. Ricardo Alfaro was recognized as Panama's president by the United States following a bloody 1931 coup led by Amulfo Arias Madrid. Alfaro served long enough to oversee Panama's peaceful 1932 elections when the people of Panama elected Harmodia Aria Madrid (Amulfo's brother) as president. Amulfo Arias Madrid came to power in 1940, but his open sympathy for fascist ideology led the military to remove him from office in October 1941, and to install Ricardo Adolfo de la Guardia as president.

The first former head of state to address the Forum, Ricardo Alfaro, president of Panama (foreground), reviews troops at Albrook Field, circa 1931-1932. Photograph courtesy of Raquel Alfaro.

Former President Alfaro spoke to the Forum on January 9, 1942, and entitled his lecture "What Will Latin America Do?" Referring to the Axis powers as "irreconcilable foe[s]," Alfaro predicted the upcoming Rio de Janeiro conference (attended by the foreign ministers of the Americas) would establish the Americas as a "military, economic and ideological unit firmly resolved to wipe Naziism from the face of the earth." Alfaro continued, "The whole of Latin America is now lined up with the United States in a demonstration of hemispherical solidarity." Unfortunately, the solidarity Alfaro spoke of was short-lived, with difficulties continuing between the United States and its Latin American neighbors throughout the last half of the twentieth century.

Beside diplomats, politicians, journalists, and educators, the Forum also welcomed to its stage the renowned clergyman Dr. S. Parkes Cadman, pastor of the Central Congregational Church, Brooklyn, New York. Cadman, who claimed a national following as a result of his Sunday afternoon radio broadcasts from the Brooklyn YMCA, addressed the Forum on February 19, 1935. The minister chose as his topic "The World at the Crossroads." A Forum audience of 1,200 squeezed into Blair Auditorium to hear the minister's lecture in which he called the United States the hope of the English-speaking world. Touching on conditions in Russia, Germany, and France, Cadman believed the United States should assist Europe, possibly as a mediator to resolve European disputes. A sampling of the questions from the audience shows the sophistication of the questions directed to the speaker: "What are the possibilities of staying out of trouble in the Far East?" "Has the war debt caused friction and bitterness?" Another question referred to the financial burden placed on Germany following the country's defeat in the Great War, a burden many historians identify as a contributing factor to the rise of fascism in Germany.

The 1943-1944 Forum season proved to be one of the most hectic in the Forum's history, with three different speakers canceling four lectures. Joseph C. Harsch (chief editor of the *Christian Science Monitor* for most of its history), canceled his January 1944 appearance most likely because he could not get away from his war correspondent duties overseas. And journalist H.H. Knickerbocker canceled his March 1944 appearance when he was forced to remain in Italy. Along with Harsch and Knickerbocker, Carlos Romulo also canceled his Forum engagement not once, but twice. However, no other speaker has gone to greater lengths to honor his engagement than did Romulo.

Winner of the 1941 Pulitzer Prize for Peace, military general, diplomat, ambassador, journalist, aide-de-camp to General Douglas MacArthur, and president of the General Assembly of the United Nations (1949-1950) are but a few of Carlos P. Romulo's lifelong accomplishments. Serving the Philippine government in exile as Secretary of Information, Romulo was originally scheduled to be the first speaker for the 1943-1944 anniversary season, an honor that passed to John Goette when Romulo was forced to cancel his appearance due to pressing matters in Washington, D.C. Romulo also canceled his second scheduled appearance set for February 13, 1944, when he was recalled to Washington, D.C., by his government. This created a rare occurrence in the history of the Forum. Left with no lecturer, the Forum was forced to cancel the evening's program.

His appearance, as already witnessed, was not easy to schedule, but finally, on Sunday, March 26, 1944, Romulo strolled onto the stage of the USO Auditorium and addressed a near capacity Forum crowd. It took a rare example of cooperation between the Forum and the leaders of the USO to hold this meeting. Since Romulo's appearance had been scheduled and canceled so many times, the Forum and the USO agreed to open the lecture to the public without charge. There were two floor sections reserved for Forum members, but members were not required to sit in these sections.

Romulo directed his remarks to the war in the Pacific. Calling the Japanese "no pushovers" and an "enemy who knows no rules," Romulo warned of a prolonged and uphill battle until the allies would be victorious, but victorious they would be, Romulo pledged. As one of the last men to escape from Bataan Island, Romulo made an impassioned plea that the events that took place on Bataan should:

   . . . be ever kept fresh in the hearts of Americans. We owe it to those heroic dead who will see no more dawns—to the living dead in concentration camps. They have faith in you. For God's sake, don't let them down.

   As far as can be determined, Romulo also received one of the highest fees paid by the Forum in those early years. His payment of $350 matched H.H. Knickerbocker's and Maurice Hindus' fees during the 1944-1945 season. It would later be eclipsed by Vincent Sheean's $500 fee in the 1945-1946 season.

   Despite its growing pains, the Forum presented a wide range of lecturers to the citizens of Norfolk. Not only did the members hear the lectures, but the greater public also "heard" the lectures through in-depth newspaper coverage. By creating a diverse dialogue, the Forum certainly lived up to its statement of intent to "promote the moral, social and educational welfare of its members." At the end of its first decade, the Norfolk Forum stood poised to move into a bright future.

This March 1945 aerial view of the Norfolk waterfront attests to its growing importance as a major port city. Photograph from the Isabella and Carroll Walker Collection; courtesy of Norfolk Public Library.

CHAPTER 4

THE BOMB, COLD WAR, AND CIVIL RIGHTS

In a 1950 editorial, the *Virginian-Pilot* wrote of the citizen's obligation to be informed on matters facing the republic. The participation of the public in a democracy, the editor argued, was necessary for the democracy's success. This responsibility had always been compelling, the writer continued, and it was greater now than at any time in history.

With the dramatic conclusion of World War II, a new era dawned in both international and domestic politics. Certainly, the Forum's membership had many questions about the bomb, the Cold War, and civil rights. To this end, the Norfolk Forum continued to ensure the public remained informed on certain pressing topics by presenting and debating a number of issues facing the nation. But there were also pressing issues facing the region, and Forum members, in their various community leadership roles, addressed these as well.

As described in Chapter Two, Norfolk possessed a less-than-stellar national reputation. Authors Thomas Parramore, Tommy Bogger and Peter Stewart, in *Norfolk: The First Four Centuries*, traced Norfolk's poor reputation to the 1890s when Norfolk was "labeled America's 'wickedest city.'" Following the 1943 *American Mercury* article, "Norfolk—Our Worst War Town," a congressional committee headed by California Representative Edouard V. M. Izac came to Norfolk to investigate the charges leveled by the *Mercury* article. The committee looked into a number of problems that had been created by the city's rapid wartime growth. Winder R. Harris, honorary Forum president, authored the Izac Committee's final report, which contained a number of recommendations covering topics as varied as venereal disease, hospital facilities, the area's food supply, Navy mess halls, transportation, parking, recreation, housing, and schools.

Even with the city pressing forward to improve its national reputation, critics remained. In 1949, the *Saturday Evening Post* cited Norfolk's rate of venereal disease (the nation's highest), the city's honky-tonks, and its three-mile slum district, and criticized Norfolk for its "too-easy social conscience."

Critics aside, Norfolk continued to shed its bawdy seaport image and remake itself into a model community. Aiding in this effort were various cultural and military organizations that helped create a more cosmopolitan city. Vivian Carter Mason founded the city's first interracial civic group, the Woman's Council For Interracial Cooperation (WCIC), in 1945. The WCIC

and the Forum shared many members, including Mrs. Louis I. (Alice) Jaffé, Mrs. Slyvan Altschul, and Mrs. A.O. Calcott, to name just a few. In 1946, I.E. Feldman, a retired Navy bandmaster, formed the Feldman Chamber Music Society, and in 1949 the city's symphony and chorus merged under the direction of Edgar Schenkman. Then, in 1952, the North Atlantic Treaty Organization (NATO) opened the Headquarters of the Supreme Allied Command, Atlantic, in Norfolk. This new NATO command brought a large number of west European military officers to the city, further enhancing the city's growing cosmopolitan atmosphere and cementing its place in the national spotlight.

The Forum, too, played a part in the city's growing national reputation. In June 1945, Charles H. Schenck, executive secretary, Chamber of Commerce, Amsterdam, New York, wrote to Forum President Lenoir Chambers inquiring about the Norfolk Forum. Amsterdam, Schenck explained, was investigating the possibility of forming a public lecture series, and had been referred to Chambers by W. Colston Leigh, Inc., a national speakers bureau that provided the bulk of Forum speakers. Schenck desired to know the nuts and bolts of how the Norfolk Forum operated. In a lengthy reply Chambers detailed membership drives, speaker arrangements, and the

Forum's internal structure. It is unknown whether Schenck's inquiry led to a public lecture series there.

By the end of the 1950s, Norfolk's renewal efforts had reaped benefits. *Look* magazine presented its Community Home Achievement Award to the city in 1957 (presented to only nine cities nationwide). In 1959, *Newsweek* prophesied that Norfolk was well on its way to becoming the "Manhattan of the South," and in 1960 Norfolk was named an All-American City.

An October 8, 1959, *Pilot* editorial remarked that the Forum had become a "firmly rooted Norfolk institution that holds well to its membership while it yearly attracts new members, notably among young people." This claim is supported by the roughly 1,400 members the Forum averaged during the 1940s and 1950s. From all indications, the Forum's lectures averaged an audience of approximately 1,000 members from the mid-1940s to the 1959-1960 season. There are, however, some indications that ticket sales slowed, but these will be addressed later.

Chambers seldom missed an opportunity to recruit new members. In 1944 he mailed twenty application forms to Mrs. A.O. Calcott, Norfolk Forum director, requesting she distribute them to friends and associates. It appears Chambers sent each director an equal number of applications, noting, "It will not be much trouble for Forum directors to do this missionary work." Chambers told the directors that there were "plenty more [applica-

Norfolk's selection as an All-American City is celebrated at this award dinner at the Arena in 1960. Photograph courtesy of Norfolk Public Library.

tions] where these came from," just in case the directors should distribute all the applications mailed initially.

In 1946 Chambers targeted a different audience. Writing to Mr. A. W. Laughton, headmaster of Norfolk Academy, Chambers enclosed a number of membership forms and requested that Laughton distribute them to his faculty. There is no evidence as to how effective these efforts were in membership recruitment.

Since its founding in 1932 the Forum had relied mainly on the citizens of Norfolk to provide the bulk of its membership rolls. For the 1955-1956 season, Forum President Harold Sugg and the board of directors urged Benjamin S. Burroughs, Membership Committee chair, to actively recruit Portsmouth residents to the rolls of the Forum. The *Ledger-Dispatch*, in a September 29, 1955, editorial, brought the public's attention to the Forum's desire to become more representative of the entire region:

The Center Theater served as the Forum's home from the late 1940s until 1972. The theater's stage hosted a number of events held especially for servicemen and women stationed in Norfolk during World War II, such as this circa 1943 concert. The renovated theater is now the Harrison Opera House. Photograph from the Isabella and Carroll Walker Collection; courtesy of Norfolk Public Library.

A special appeal is being made this year for memberships in Portsmouth, with a view to making the Forum an agency for the whole area if a sufficient number of Portsmouth memberships is obtained.

The special attention given to Portsmouth bore fruit. The Forum's Portsmouth contingent increased from 69 members (1954-1955 season) to 180 for the 1955-1956 season. This growth led Burroughs to publicly announce the Forum's consideration of adding a fifth lecture—at no additional cost—to the Forum's 1956-1957 season. Initial plans were to hold this lecture at Portsmouth's Woodrow Wilson High School if enough interest remained the following year. Once again, there is no evidence that this proposal became anything more than just that, a proposal.

A final indicator that ticket sales slowed can be found in the time of year tickets remained available to the public. Early in the Forum's history, membership drives were held, as today, during the spring months of April, May, and June, with the yearly membership quota often being filled within a fortnight of the public offering. Beginning in the mid-1940s and lasting through the 1950s, Forum memberships were regularly available as late as September and October. For example, the letters containing Forum membership applications posted by Chambers to Calcott and Laughton were both dated in September. A week prior to the first lecture of the 1950-1951 season Forum President Joseph A. Leslie, Jr., urged "prospective patrons" to send in their application requests. The announcement of Judge Harold R. Medina's lecture to start the 1955-1956 season noted season tickets would be available at the door on the night of his lecture. In September 1957, the Forum announced that 1,500 subscriptions had been sold, but the membership drive remained underway. Finally, the October 10, 1959, *Pilot* announced the Forum's membership quota of 1,800 had just been reached.

While tickets may not have sold at the same brisk rate of earlier years, a high demand for season tickets still existed. This demand necessitated moving the Forum's lectures into the 1,800-seat Center Theater on a permanent basis in 1947. This allowed the Forum to increase the number of yearly memberships available and may explain, in part, the availability of tickets so close to the season's first lecture in the 1950s. The Forum remained at the Center Theater until it moved into the newly opened Chrysler Hall in 1972.

Not only did the Forum grow in numbers, its reputation also grew as well. In 1952, the *Pilot* editorialized that the Forum had been "established to present public discussion . . . serv[ing] no man's cause—and every man's." In a May 12, 1954, *Pilot* article, the Forum was characterized as one of Norfolk's "most important organizations." An October 8, 1959, *Pilot* editorial referred to the Forum as a "firmly rooted Norfolk institution" that has been "lifting Norfolk's horizons . . . for more than 25 years." High praise for the Forum from the newspapers is not surprising, given the number of newspapermen who served in a leadership capacity in the Forum.

But perhaps the most poignant example of the Forum's standing in the eyes of the community can be found in a letter from Augusta S. Goodman to Lenoir Chambers dated July 30, 1946. Goodman's letter dealt with the Cavalier Beach Club's policy of barring Jews from club membership. Goodman hoped Chambers, because of his position as editor of the *Ledger-Dispatch* and his "leadership and support of the Norfolk Forum," would "see fit to bring a speaker who is really top-notch on the subject [anti-Semitism]." A review of the speakers for several years following 1946, however, does not indicate whether the Forum booked any lecturers on this topic.

Personal ties with the rich and famous have been a source of many speakers for the Forum. Here Charles T. Abeles (right), former Forum president, and Mrs. Abeles greet Senator Leverett Saltonstall in April 1950. Saltonstall and Abeles attended Harvard University and were teammates on Harvard's crew. Photograph courtesy of Norfolk Public Library.

As in the Forum's first decade, there remained considerable continuity in the leadership of the Forum. Cherry Nottingham continued to serve the Forum in a variety of positions, including board of directors, secretary, vice-president, and honorary vice-president, until her death in 1965. Robert C. de Rosset served as the Forum's treasurer from 1945 to 1951. De Rosset, a vice-president of the Seaboard Citizens National Bank, had served as co-chair of the Norfolk War Finance Committee and two of the city's War Loan Campaigns. Stockton H. Tyler, Jr., began a twenty-year tenure as the Forum's treasurer in 1955. A lifelong resident of the Norfolk area, Tyler began his career in banking with the Seaboard Citizens National Bank and served as senior vice-president of Seaboard's successor, Crestar Bank. Just like many previous Forum leaders, Tyler was active in many aspects of his community, serving on a number of boards ranging from the Medical Center Hospital to Berkley Machine and Iron Works.

Charles T. Abeles succeeded Chambers as president and served in this capacity for four years (1946-1949). A twin and one of seven boys, Abeles was born in St. Louis, Missouri, on July 22, 1891. He graduated from Smith Academy, a private school, in 1907, before matriculating to Harvard University. Abeles obtained his B.A. in 1913 and law degree in 1916. He returned to St. Louis and, gaining admission to the Missouri Bar, began practice as an associate of the law firm of Boyle and Priest. When the United States declared war on the Central Powers, he enlisted in the Navy and was assigned to patrol work in Norfolk. Abeles' naval career led, indirectly, to his career with the Seaboard Airline Railway. He was appointed an attorney for the railway located in Norfolk when he left the Navy in 1919.

Norfolk's legal community quickly recognized Abeles' abilities, and he was soon considered to be one of the city's top lawyers. In 1926 Abeles became a solicitor with Seaboard, and in 1943 he became a senior general attorney for the company. In 1956 Abeles became Seaboard's general solicitor. He served as the head of the legal department until his retirement in 1961.

Turner Dozier, writing for *New Norfolk* in May 1965, described Abeles as a man with "quiet confidence, tact, [and] sensitivity." The *Ledger-Star,* in a tribute editorial following Abeles' death in March 1980, characterized him as "Genial in manner, generous with his time and talents . . . [who] had an effective hand in a remarkable array of community activities." Following in the footsteps of previous Forum leaders, Abeles gave to his community in a number of ways, including as chairman of the Norfolk Commission on Higher Education during the early 1950s, director of the Norfolk Museum of Arts and Sciences, and as the executive director of the Norfolk Foundation in 1963. In the late 1960s, Abeles served as chairman of the Chamber of Commerce Roads and Bridges Committee which oversaw the development of what is now Waterside Drive.

The Norfolk Forum and the *Virginian-Pilot* have had a long relationship. Pictured here are Pulitzer Prize winner Lenoir Chambers (center), Forum president 1943-1946, and Frank Batten, Forum board of directors member 1956 (right). Also pictured is Managing Editor Robert Mason (left). Photograph courtesy of the *Virginian-Pilot.*

Abeles' length of tenure as Forum president (1946-1949) is second only to J.E. Capps' five years of service (1933-1937), and just ahead of Winder Harris' three years (1938-1940). Harris resigned the presidency at the beginning of his fourth term as president in 1941, following his election to Congress. Chambers also served three years as president, from 1943 to 1945. These four men—Chambers, Harris, Capps, and Abeles—served as president of the Norfolk Forum for fifteen of the Forum's first eighteen years. A remarkably steady course had been steered by these four men during the Forum's formative years.

During Abeles' administration, the Forum underwent several changes. In 1949, possibly as a result of the length of service that Chambers, Abeles, Capps, and Harris provided, the board of directors explored placing term limits on officers, and implementing a rotation plan for the board. Presidents of the Forum, for the most part from this point on, served one two-year term; however other constitutional offices do not seem to have been as constricted as the presidency at this point, for example, the twenty years Stockton H. Tyler, Jr., served as the Forum's treasurer.

The board of directors rotation plan required that at least a third of

the directors rotate off the board every three years. The plan divided the board into three groups: one to serve for three years, a second for two years, and a third group to serve only one year. In any case, an individual could serve on the board of directors for a maximum of three years. Following the third consecutive year as a board member, the director would be forced to take a one-year sabbatical prior to serving on the board again. This rotation plan was adopted in 1950 and implemented in 1951; it continues today.

The decision made by Abeles' administration to move the Forum's lectures into the Center Theater precipitated a price increase. While the larger Center Theater allowed the Forum to increase its membership, it also increased the yearly cost of renting the lecture facility. In 1947, the year of the move, the cost of a Forum membership rose to $2.00, and for the 1950-1951 season, ticket prices went to $2.50. The cost of a season ticket remained at $2.50 until the 1958-1959 season when the price increased to $3.00.

Joseph A. Leslie, Jr., and Harold G. Sugg added to the growing number of local newspaper editors active in the Norfolk Forum. Leslie served as the Forum's president for two years (1950-1951). He had assumed editorial leadership of the *Ledger-Dispatch* following Chambers' return to the *Virginian-Pilot* in 1950. Born in southwest Virginia, Leslie differed from a number of previous Forum officers. While Jaffé, Chambers, and Calcott, for example, worked for moderation and tolerance in race relations, Leslie tended to be a traditionalist when it came to race relations in the South. This ideological division can clearly be seen in the editorial positions Chambers and Leslie advocated during Virginia's Massive Resistance movement following the Supreme Court's 1954 *Brown v. Board of Education* decision. Chambers' editorials opposed Massive Resistance, while Leslie's strongly worded editorials supported resistance and the maintenance of a segregat-

From its beginning, starting with charter member Louis I. Jaffé, the Forum's leadership from the ranks of the *Pilot* has also included Winder Harris, Joseph A. Leslie, Jr. (left), Harold Sugg (below), William Meacham (right), Frank Batten, Jr., Guy Friddell, and Glenn Scott (far right). Photographs courtesy of the *Virginian-Pilot*.

ed public school system. In the end, Chambers became the second *Virginian-Pilot* editor and second Forum member to receive the Pulitzer Prize for editorial writing, continuing the tradition established by Louis I. Jaffé.

Harold G. Sugg, an associate editor at the *Virginian-Pilot*, served as president of the Norfolk Forum for two years (1954-1955). Sugg hailed from Greenville, North Carolina, and was a graduate of Davidson College. He

joined the *Pilot* as a reporter in 1939, and became an associate editor under Chambers in 1950. Sugg supported Chambers' anti-Massive Resistance editorial stance. In 1957, he became an assistant publisher of the newspaper. Two new board members continue the long-standing association with the *Virginian-Pilot* and Landmark Communications, the newspaper's parent company. Jennifer Sanford, a Landmark staff member, recently joined the Forum board. Her mother, Jeannette Blount, who passed away in 1998, was the Forum's secretary from 1991 to 1996. Donald Patterson, executive vice-president of Landmark and president of their broadcasting company, began his first Forum board term in 1998.

A number of local judges also served in leadership roles for the Forum. Richard B. Spindle, Norfolk Police Court Justice, served as a board member during the late 1940s. Likewise judges Thomas M. Johnson, William Moultrie Guerry, and Walter Page also served on the Forum's board during the 1940s and 1950s. The board's most recent directors have included judges Lydia Calvert Taylor, Everett Martin, Jr., Thomas S. Shadrick, and Rebecca Beach Smith. No other judge, however, achieved the national profile or reputation of future Federal District Court judge and Forum board of directors member (1949-1950) Walter E. Hoffman.

A lifelong republican, Hoffman was born in Jersey City, New Jersey. He received a degree in economics from the University of Pennsylvania in 1928, and after attending law school at the College of William and Mary Hoffman received his law degree from Washington and Lee University in 1931. Hoffman, along with

Edward L. Breeden, Jr., then established a law practice in Norfolk. Following an unsuccessful campaign against Porter Hardy, Jr., for the Second Congressional District house seat in 1948, Hoffman stood for the office of state attorney general on the Republican ticket headed by Ted Dalton in 1952. In a remarkable showing against Senator Harry Flood Byrd's political machine, the Dalton ticket garnered 45 percent of the vote.

President Dwight D. Eisenhower appointed Hoffman to the federal bench in 1954. Hoffman soon established a reputation as a no-nonsense but extremely fair judge. He was selected to preside over the grand jury investigation of then Vice-President Spiro T. Agnew in 1973. Guy Friddell, writing in the November 25, 1996, *Pilot*, reported that Attorney General Elliott Richardson attempted to solicit a pledge from Hoffman that the judge would not sentence Agnew to prison if he was convicted on bribery charges. Hoffman, Friddell writes, refused to agree with this demand, which led the administration to work out a complex plea bargain with Agnew.

In 1957 two cases were brought by the National Association for the Advancement of Colored People—*Adkins v. School Board of the City of Newport News* and *Beckett v. School Board of the City of Norfolk*—to challenge the constitutionality of the state's pupil placement law. They were combined into a single case to be heard by Judge Hoffman. In his decision Hoffman ruled the state's pupil placement law unconstitutional. He wrote that the state could not assign students to a school based solely on the student's race, thus paving the way for Norfolk's schools to be integrated.

Judge Hoffman also left another legacy. His son, Walter Hoffman, Jr., is an active Forum member who has served in a number of Forum offices, including president.

Roy B. Martin, Jr., was also a man of principle who served on the board of directors of the Forum throughout the 1950s and the early 1960s. A native Norfolkian, Martin was born on May 13, 1921, and attended public schools in Norfolk prior to graduating from the Norfolk Division of the College of William and Mary in 1940, and the University of Virginia in 1943. Martin, appointed by Norfolk Mayor Fred W. Duckworth to fill a vacant city council seat in 1953, went on to become the mayor of Norfolk in 1962 and served until 1974. It was Martin who made the first public split with Duckworth over Massive Resistance.

In January 1959, Duckworth proposed that city council close all grades, white and black, above the sixth grade. According to Forrest P. White, in his insightful account of Norfolk's school closing, *Pride and Prejudice: School Desegregation and Urban Renewal in Norfolk, 1950-1959*, this action would lock out an additional 1,914 whites and 5,529 blacks from Norfolk's public schools. Martin stood alone in opposing this action when, in the words of White, he "caused a ripple of surprise and then applause from the pro-school advocates" with his "no" vote. As has been seen with other Forum leaders such as Chambers and Hoffman, Martin, in an act that White called "raw political courage," stood alone as the only city councilman to oppose the school closing.

Following Martin's public defiance, other Forum members voiced their opposition to the school closing. Mason C. Andrews (Forum member), Benjamin S. Burroughs (board member), R.O. Davis (Forum president 1956-1957), C. Wiley Grandy, IV (Forum member), Samuel T. Northern (board member and former treasurer), Richard B. Spindle, III (Forum president 1958-1959), Michael B. Wagenheim (former vice-president and board member), and Thomas H. Willcox (former vice-president and board member), endorsed the Committee of One Hundred's public petition urging that the city's schools be reopened. Consisting of prominent business and community leaders, the Committee of One Hundred's petition, spearheaded by Henry Clay Hofheimer II, was published in the *Pilot* on January 27, 1959. This public action was taken, as was the case with Judge Hoffman, at great personal risk.

The Forum's role also boasted strong-minded, talented women. Besides Cherry Nottingham, a number of other women served on the Forum's board of directors and as Forum officers. Virginia Lynn Tunstall served on the Forum's board throughout the 1940s and 1950s. A rather well known poet, Tunstall had her work published in *Contemporary Verse*, the *Lyric*, the *Boston Transcript*, and a number of other literary journals. Tunstall's *A White Sail Set*, published in 1927, featured poems inspired by the greater Tidewater area.

Mrs. A.O. Calcott again demonstrates the public spirit found throughout the Forum's membership. The Business and Professional

Woman's Club recognized Calcott for her service to Norfolk in 1939 by presenting her with the club's first Outstanding Woman Award. She also served on the Norfolk School Board, and as president of the Norfolk Anti-Tuberculosis League. Calcott became only the second woman to receive the Cosmopolitan Club's Distinguished Service Award when she was selected as Norfolk's outstanding citizen in 1945. Calcott's service extended beyond Norfolk as well. Educated by private tutors, she was appointed by Governor Colgate W. Darden (a Forum co-founder) to the board of visitors of the University of Virginia in 1944, and received the Distinguished Service Certificate from the State School Trustees Association shortly thereafter.

Like other early founders of the Forum, Calcott worked for tolerance and understanding between all peoples, and possessed a passion for public affairs. As a member of the WCIC, Calcott served as the council's representative to the Norfolk City Federation of Home and School Leagues, and the Parent-Teacher Association. Calcott was also a founding member of the Portsmouth Forum, and served as vice-president of that organization sometime prior to 1945.

The Norfolk Forum's goal was then, and continues to be now, to bring speakers to the city who can provide insight into the issues of public concern. The end of the Second World War saw a shift in the selection of lecturers. The world of journalism continued to produce the majority of Forum speakers; however, more scientists, entertainers, even spies, graced the Forum's stage. The Forum also presented its second former head of state, and the first of three former British prime ministers to its membership, as we shall see.

As the variety of speakers increased, so too did their topics. While Asian and European affairs and the World War had dominated the first decade of the Forum's lectures, the Cold War, in the broadest sense of the term, dominated the next decade and a half. There were other topics presented to the Forum as well. These ranged from general entertainment, economics and space exploration, to labor-management relations, political corruption, and India's independence, to name just a few.

At least four speakers addressed the Forum on some aspect of life in the atomic age between 1944 and 1959. Vincent Sheean, a war correspondent and author, addressed the Forum on October 11, 1945, arguing that the United States could not keep atomic weapon manufacturing secrets secret for much longer, a prediction that proved to be accurate. The United States maintained its monopoly on nuclear weapons from 1945 until September 1949, when Truman announced the Soviet Union had detonated an atomic weapon. Sheean also asserted that atomic weapons were having a negative influence on the foreign policy of the United States by annoying and upsetting the Soviet Union.

Time magazine science editor, Dr. Gerald Wendt, addressed the Forum on October 8, 1946, and chose as his topic, "Science of the Future Against the Background of the Atomic Age." Wendt predicted that the atomic bomb had been used for the first and the last time in the last war. But he recognized the possibility that the weapons could be used as a tool of "mass poisoning." Wendt, nonetheless, saw a silver lining in the atomic cloud and predicted that domestic nuclear energy would prove to be a safe, efficient, continuous supply of electricity for the future. This new energy source, Wendt believed, would change the American lifestyle more in the upcoming decade than any other invention had over the last fifty years, a prediction that did not quite turn out as Wendt hoped.

Dr. David Bradley also addressed the dangers of atomic secrecy, but from a slightly different perspective. Bradley had served in the United States Army and was a witness to atomic weapons tests conducted at Bikini Atoll in the South Pacific. Bradley's log during his tour with Operation Crossroads from May to October 1946, was published in 1948 under the title *No Place to Hide* in 1948. Appearing before the Forum on January 19, 1950, shortly after the disclosure of the United States hydrogen bomb program, Bradley argued that the atomic secrecy program had driven scientists out of atomic research by bogging them down in bureaucratic red tape.

Finally, Dr. Ralph E. Lapp, director of the Nuclear Science Service and former member of the Manhattan Project, addressed an audience of 1,000 Forum members on March 29, 1955. Lapp referred to Winston Churchill's belief that peace could be maintained by nuclear weapons "through mutual terror," a belief that became known as "mutual assured destruction." While Lapp believed the current crises in the Matsu and Quemoy Islands could "trigger . . . us into atomic war," he contended that "the miraculous will to survive" found in humans would deter any future use of nuclear weapons. Lapp's second address would occur in 1962 during the greatest nuclear showdown the world has yet witnessed: the Cuban Missile Crisis.

Other aspects of the Cold War drew attention also. The Marshall Plan, a multi-billion-dollar program to rebuild western Europe, was developed by the State Department's Policy Planning Staff for Secretary of State George Marshall. Unveiled in June 1947, at Harvard University, Marshall warned that continued American prosperity depended on a quick economic recovery in Europe. Expansion of the European economy, the United States believed, would negate any further growth of Communism.

The Marshall Plan was the topic of two consecutive speakers in the spring of 1948. James Bellah, American author, speaking on America's foreign policy, referred to the Marshall Plan as something "Americans must carry out for their self-preservation." In his April 6, 1948, speech, Herbert Agar, editor of the *Louisville Courier-Journal* and Pulitzer Prize winner, called the Marshall Plan a decent, generous, and wise program that would show that Karl Marx's ideology was wrong and that the United States' ideology was right. Agar urged that there be no limit on expenditures to Europe under the Marshall Plan "because we have taken under the rehabilitation of man."

The domestic front of the Cold War was not ignored by Forum lecturers. Herbert Philbrick, a former Federal Bureau of Investigation domestic counterespionage agent, addressed the Forum on April 8, 1953. Philbrick,

British Prime Minister Clement Attlee (left) and former Prime Minister Winston Churchill share a carriage during a World War II victory parade. *New York Times* photograph courtesy of the National Archives.

author of *I Led Three Lives*, spent nine years as a member of the Communist Party while an agent of the FBI. Philbrick infiltrated the Communist Party in 1940 when he unknowingly joined a civic group in Cambridge, Massachusetts, that was an alleged Communist Party front. According to Philbrick he rose to the position of chairman prior to learning of the group's ties to the Communist Party. Philbrick left his undercover work in 1949 when the government called him as a surprise witness in the trial of the so-called Communist Eleven. Philbrick continued to testify against alleged communists right up to his appearance before the Forum in 1953. On the Tuesday of the week Philbrick appeared on the Forum's stage, he testified before the Senate Internal Security Subcommittee that five current Boston ministers were "disciplined members of the Red underground."

The trial of the Communist Eleven, the nation's top Communist Party members, was presided over by Federal District Court Judge Harold Medina. Judge Medina spoke to the Forum on October 25, 1955, before a near capacity crowd. The judge argued Americans wanted "a leadership they can trust and they [wished to] uphold the American heritage of goodwill, freedom and justice." Medina asserted that the "lawyers for the Commies" used the trial to "spread Communist propaganda" and disrupt the trial. Medina asserted that this tactic was an attempt by the Communists to make a mockery of the American judicial system. In so doing the Communists hoped to show the legal system had no right to try them. Medina believed that if their tactics had been successful, it would have led to a Communist victory on the domestic front. The trial resulted in the conviction of all eleven men on charges of conspiracy to advocate overthrowing the government by violence. They received jail sentences of three to five years each.

The Forum did not limit its interest in spies to the Cold War's domestic front. Nicol Smith, former organizer of the underground in Siam, spoke of his life as an American secret agent working for the Office of Strategic Services (OSS) during the war. Rear Admiral E.M. Zacharias, United States Navy intelligence officer and author of *Secret Missions: The Story of an Intelligence Officer*, addressed the Forum in October 1947.

Earl Clement R. Attlee, former British prime minister, graced the Forum stage on February 8, 1960. Succeeding Winston Churchill, Attlee became prime minister on July 26, 1945, serving until his Labour Party's defeat in the 1951 elections. Under Attlee's leadership Great Britain joined NATO, the Council of Europe for unity of the European peoples, and, in what Attlee considered his greatest accomplishment, granted India its independence.

During his lecture, Attlee urged a policy of reconciliation toward the Communist block nations. Addressing the Forum on "The Future of Europe," Attlee urged the West to learn to "live with Communists 'as fellow citizens of the world,'" according to the *Pilot*. Like other Forum speakers before him, Attlee believed the world would "avoid destroying" itself "by bombs or allowing it to be corrupted by false doctrines." This

British Prime Minister Clement Attlee (left) enjoys a break on the final day of the Berlin Conference on August 1, 1945. Pictured with Attlee are President Harry S. Truman (center) and Generalissimo Josef Stalin (right). Army Signal Corps photograph; courtesy of the National Archives.

could be accomplished, Attlee argued, by living and associating with Communists to show them the "conceptions" of the West "are truer than theirs."

Not all Forum lectures during this period were of such a serious nature. It was during this time the Forum began a subtle shift away from such serious matters by booking a greater number of entertainers. Walter Crawford Kelly, creator of the *Pogo* cartoon strip, addressed the Forum on November 17, 1953. The *Pilot* wrote that "interest was apparent among the bleak ranks of sophisticates" who attended the lecture. Kelly spoke on the history of the comic strip, which began with the ancient Egyptians, during the first half of his presentation. The second portion of his lecture Kelly devoted to drawing and explaining the principal characters of the strip.

Prior to Kelly's address that evening, a reception in his honor was held at the home of Mr. and Mrs. C. (Cyrus) Wiley Grandy, IV. Grandy would serve the Forum as second vice-president beginning in 1966. His wife Ann was also a member of the board. Their daughter Carter remembers attending a number of Forum receptions held at the Grandy home when she was growing up. At the reception for Kelly, he drew one of his cartoons just for Carter. The cartoon still hangs in the home of that young girl, now long-time Forum member and former Forum President Carter Grandy Scott.

The poet Ogden Nash addressed a capacity Forum audience on February 22, 1955. Nash's topic, "Mid-way Through Nash," explored the question, "What would happen . . . if a person who knew the rules wrote bad poetry purposely rather than unconsciously?" Examples of Nash's deliberately poor poetry can be found in "Candy is dandy, but liquor is quicker," the only poem Nash believed would outlive him. The Forum audience received a special treat when Nash read, for the first time in public, an anti-nuclear weapon poem he claimed had been turned down by every publisher to whom it had been submitted. The poem's setting was the interior of the Museum of Natural History, and its characters were a number of dancing fossils. One fossil says to the author, following an evening of dancing, "Cheer up old man," as he winked, "It's kind of fun to be extinct."

The poet Louis Untermeyer spoke to the Forum December 1, 1959, on "What's New in the American Arts?" Appearing before a "near-capacity house," according to the review, Untermeyer spoke highly of American arts by pointing out that the world's architects, painters, musicians, and authors now look toward America for their inspiration. Untermeyer, Harold Sugg noted, had never graduated from high school. Always prepared with a witty retort, Untermeyer replied, "Euclid had his angles and I had mine."

Agna Enters, dance mime, painter, sculptor, and author, replaced Edith Atwater and Albert Dekker when they were unable to honor their January 21, 1958, Forum engagement. The *Virginian-Pilot* article announcing her appearance credited her with the creation of the dance mime. The mime, according to the article, combines "for the first time the arts of mime, dances, choreography, costume and scenic design and, if necessary, music compositions." Enters' appearance before the Forum might have been the group's most unique up to that point.

No less than three Forum lecturers addressed the issue of India's independence during the 1940s and 1950s. Appearing November 21, 1944, T.A. Raman, a former journalist and then current Government of India Information Service staff member in the United States, spoke on "India, Today and Tomorrow." Arranged through the efforts of Chambers, with the assistance of James Guthrie, British consulate in Norfolk, Raman addressed India's future postwar independence. Britain had promised to make India a free and equal partner in the British Empire within eighteen months of the conclusion of World War II. Raman believed the division between Mahatma K. Gandhi's Congress Party and the Moslem League would soon be solved, clearing the way for the British to honor their promise, and grant India its independence.

The next speaker to address the Forum on India was Lady Rama Rau, wife of Sir Benegal Rau, the former Indian ambassador to the United States. Before a Forum audience on October 21, 1953, Lady Rau lectured on "India's

Social Revolution." Lady Rau outlined the efforts taken by India over several decades to gain their independence, an independence that India did not achieve until 1947 following Gandhi's program of civil disobedience. Unlike other political movements, Rau noted, which had been led by elite intellectuals, Gandhi's leadership had been spiritual in nature, with the idea of freedom applying to everyone, including the untouchables.

Finally Madam Vijaya L. Pandit, sister of Indian Prime Minister Jawaharlal Nehru, addressed the Forum in its opening session of the 1959-1960 season. Madam Pandit spoke on "India's Foreign Policy," and targeted the India-China border dispute for the bulk of her remarks. However, one remark remains particularly compelling: "If we in India . . . can convert democracy from a political creed to a way of life, then peace can be saved."

In this fifteen-year period of the Forum's history, the world, the nation, the state, and the city faced difficult and demanding questions. Questions covering atomic weapons and the Cold War were addressed with regularity. At the opposite end, entertainers became more prominent on the Forum's schedule. Following the peaceful reopening of Norfolk's schools, the city took a deep collective breath and settled down, wondering what lay ahead in the coming decade.

Pogo creator Walter Crawford Kelly drew this panel of the famous character and dedicated it to "Magna Carter," now Carter Grandy Scott. Cartoon courtesy of Carter Grandy Scott.

The Center Theater served as the Forum's home from the mid-1940s
until 1972. Photograph courtesy of Harrison Opera House.

CHAPTER 5

ONE STEP BACK,
TWO STEPS FORWARD

Norfolk and the region continued their self-improvement efforts throughout the restless sixties, inflationary seventies, and the Reagan eighties. Beginning with the 1960s, Norfolk's growth was aided when the city lost more of its geographic isolation with the opening of the Midtown Tunnel (1963) and the Chesapeake Bay Bridge-Tunnel (1964). The Hampton Roads Bridge Tunnel had been in operation since the late 1950s. With greater access came a number of opportunities. In 1961 the Medical Tower at Norfolk General Hospital opened, and in 1964 Dr. Mason C. Andrews, future Forum board member, spearheaded formation of the Norfolk Area Medical Center Authority. The authority was dedicated to creating a major medical teaching complex in Norfolk. After nearly ten years of work, the goal became a reality with the opening of Eastern Virginia Medical School.

The city's art scene also continued to improve. Norfolk's Little Theater opened in the summer of 1965, providing theatergoers with summer stage entertainment. The Norfolk Arts Festival began in 1961. And perhaps most importantly, the Norfolk Museum of Arts and Sciences merged with the Chrysler Museum in Provincetown, Massachusetts, and was thereafter known as the Chrysler Museum, in accordance with benefactors Walter P. Chrysler, Jr., and his wife, Norfolk native Jean Outland Chrysler. Norfolk Mayor Roy Martin arranged for the city to fund a one-million-dollar addition to the museum in the Chrysler family's honor. Finally, in 1972, Chrysler Hall opened. A 2,500-seat, state-of-the-art concert hall, it became home to the Norfolk Forum in October 1972, with a lecture by columnist and Brandies University Professor Max Lerner.

Unlike the city, the Forum faced a difficult and uncertain future. For the first time in its history membership seems to have waned between 1960 and 1985. The long-time home of the Forum, the Center Theater, seated 1,800 patrons for a Forum lecture; however, during the 1960-1961 season, membership peaked at only 1,702. By mid-October 1963, only two-thirds of the available seats had been reserved by Forum patrons. The gap between seats and sales was even wider when you bear in mind the principle the Forum leadership learned in the early 1930s: all members will not attend every lecture and therefore seating can be oversold by an average of ten percent, a goal the Forum had regularly reached prior to this time.

Exactly why the Forum experienced such a downturn in its membership is not clear. Arguably the 1960s and the early 1970s, with the exception

of the Civil War, were the most turbulent years in the nation's domestic existence, including the Cold War and nuclear threat, Vietnam, civil rights struggles, assassinations and, for the first time in the nation's history, the forced resignation of both a sitting vice-president and president. Perhaps Norfolkians were too worried about their immediate needs to consider the intellectual ponderings offered by the Forum.

Or, perhaps, as board member Gene Justice pointed out during a conversation with the author, younger adults influenced by the events of the 1960s and 1970s did not feel comfortable joining such an "establishment" organization. Former Forum president J. Hume Taylor (1971-1972) once commented, after looking out over the audience from the Forum's stage, that it could be wiped out by one good flu epidemic.

In an effort to boost ticket sales for the 1965-1966 season, the Forum made season tickets available for purchase at the Center Theater's box office. This appears to be the first time since the 1934-1935 season that tickets were available to potential subscribers other than by mail order and the occasional opening night. The greater accessibility to tickets does not appear to have increased sales. Season tickets were still available at the Center's box office the night of the first lecture.

This downward trend appears to have continued throughout the decade. In December 1968, when announcing the election of *Virginian-Pilot* editor Glenn Scott to the presidency of the Forum, the newspaper reported the Forum's membership at 1,400 for the current season. Scott confirmed in a later interview the difficulty the Forum experienced in maintaining members. "When I became president the Forum was having a lean year. In fact, the Forum often had difficulty selling out."

As the Forum moved into the 1970s, membership numbers, unlike inflation, do not appear to have increased. In November 1970, membership stood at an amazingly low 1,025 members. And at the beginning of the 1979-1980 program, season tickets were also still available at the Center Theater's box office prior to the season's first two lectures.

In an effort to decrease the number of non-renewing members, the Forum leadership took direct action. Under the leadership of Forum presidents Dr. Willcox Ruffin, Jr. (1981-1982), and Allan Donn (1983-1984), working with Ticket Sales Committee Chairman Jim Matthews, a telemarketing strategy was devised to ensure current subscribers renewed their membership. In a letter to the board of directors dated October 5, 1983, Donn announced that while tickets sales stood at 1,312 ("approximately 300 tickets ahead of our position at the comparable date last season"), a recruitment meeting would be held at the law firm of Willcox, Savage, Dickson, Hillis, and Eley, P.C., on October 17. The purpose of this special meeting was to contact non-renewing season ticket holders by phone and urge them to renew their subscriptions. According to Donn's letter, "A similar one-night effort last year" proved very successful. The direct marketing effort seems to have had some success, with a season membership of 1,836 members for the 1983-1984 season, and 1,710 members for the 1985-1986 season.

Vice Admiral R.O. Davis is but one example of United States Navy participation in the Norfolk Forum. Photograph courtesy of the National Archives.

In spite of the most difficult time in the Forum's history, the leadership remained dedicated to the Forum and to public service, in the tradition of the Forum's early leaders. Like members Winder R. Harris, Porter Hardy, Jr., Norman Hamilton, and Colgate Darden, Jr., before him, Forum President G. William Whitehurst won election to Congress from Norfolk's Second Congressional District in November 1968. While his congressional career was lengthy (1969-1987), Whitehurst served the shortest tenure of any Forum president, from May to December 1968.

As with previous Forum leaders, Whitehurst served in the armed forces. Whitehurst was a United States Navy combat aircrewman during World War II. During his entire stay in Congress (1969-1987), Whitehurst served on the House Armed Services Committee. With the region's strong ties to the military, perhaps no other congressional committee is more important to the area.

Naval officers have been active in the Forum from its founding, which seems only natural for an organization operating in a city so tied to that service. Rear Admiral H.O. Stickney, Commandant, Fifth Naval District, accompanied Ober and others to the May 1932 meeting with FPA representative William T. Stone. Retired Vice Admiral R.O. Davis, former Commandant, Fifth Naval District, served a two-year term as president of the Forum beginning in 1956. Vice Admiral Ira Nunn served on the Forum's board of directors in 1958, along with Rear Admiral James H. Ward. Rear Admiral Hugh C. Haynesworth, Commanding Officer, Naval Supply Center, replaced Ward in 1959. More recently, Admiral Paul David Miller, Commander in Chief, U.S. Atlantic Fleet, served on the board of the Norfolk Forum.

The military has also provided the Forum with a number of speakers. The first military officer to address the Forum was retired Rear Admiral E.M. Zacharias on October 13, 1947. As mentioned previously, Zacharias authored *Secret Missions: The Story of an Intelligence Officer*. He had recently retired from active service, having been involved in, as the *Virginian-Pilot* phrased it, "the recent softening up of Japan." Zacharias was followed by retired Admiral Louis E. Denfeld, former Chief of Naval Operations, on October 26, 1950. As might be expected Denfeld attacked the specter of Communism, calling for the United States to maintain a large and powerful peacetime navy, a plea certain to have fallen on receptive Norfolk ears. United States Air Force Brigadier General Robert L. Scott (Ret.) addressed the Forum on April 18, 1961, on "The Struggle for Supremacy in Space."

On February 2, 1972, Admiral Elmo R. Zumwalt, Jr., Chief of Naval Operations and originator of the infamous messages dubbed "Z-grams," challenged the United States not to lose its naval supremacy to the Soviet Union. Zumwalt cited a recent Soviet worldwide naval exercise that included 150 surface ships, 50 submarines, and hundreds of aircraft as an example of the Soviet threat to the United States Navy.

Two former United States Navy Chiefs of Naval Operations have spoken before the Forum: Admiral Louis Denfeld (left) and Admiral Elmo R. Zumwalt, Jr. (below). Photographs courtesy of the Navy Historical Center.

Finally, United States Army General and former Chairman of the Joint Chiefs of Staff, Colin Powell, addressed a sold-out Forum on Tuesday, September 20, 1994, following his return from a peace mission to Haiti with former President James E. "Jimmy" Carter and United States Senator Sam Nunn. Carter's peace mission, to avoid armed United States intervention into Haiti's domestic problems, succeeded when, on Sunday, September 18, a settlement was reached with the Haitian government in the final hours preceding the invasion.

Ascending to the presidency of the Forum (1968-1971) following Whitehurst's election to Congress, Glenn Scott continued the long associa-

Thomas Shuttleworth (third from left), then Forum president, and his wife Marian (left) accompany General Colin Powell to the home of Oriana and Arnold McKinnon (right) who hosted a reception in the general's honor the night of his lecture on September 20, 1994. Powell had recently returned from a peace mission with former President Jimmy Carter to Haiti. Photograph courtesy of Thomas Shuttleworth.

tion between *Virginian-Pilot* editors and the Norfolk Forum. Scott joined the staff of the *Virginian-Pilot* in the late 1950s as acting book editor, replacing Malissa Childs-Redfield (daughter of noted columnist Marquis W. Childs) who accompanied her husband on a tour of duty in Europe.

Malissa Childs-Redfield obtained her position with the *Pilot* as an indirect result of her father's first appearance before the Forum. A large Forum audience turned out on January 6, 1948, to hear Marquis W. Childs call Henry A. Wallace's third party presidential bid tragic and harmful to the nation. Having met Lenoir Chambers while in Norfolk, Childs struck up and maintained a correspondence with Chambers during the latter years of the

1940s, and on February 1, 1956, Childs renewed his correspondence with Chambers: "I am presuming on our brief meeting of some years back when I spoke in Norfolk (Childs'appearance before the Forum) to ask if you would do a kindness for me." The kindness Childs requested was for Chambers to explore the possibility of Malissa gaining employment with the *Pilot*. On November 15, 1960, Childs, perhaps as a return favor, once again addressed the Forum. According to the *Virginian-Pilot*, Childs called for a "superior effort" to be made to end the nuclear arms race and predicted that, in fifty years, President Dwight D. Eisenhower would be remembered as a great military leader and not as president.

It was during Scott's administration that the Forum (from evidence on hand) first reached out to Norfolk's African American community, focusing on the region's education system. Scott recalls that under his leadership, Forum programs and membership applications were taken to Norfolk State University and placed in professors' and administrators' mail boxes in order to attract African American members. Unfortunately, according to Scott, this effort was met with a less than enthusiastic response. Scott also recounted a similar attempt to recruit members from the city's African American public school teachers. Once again, according to Scott, the Forum's efforts were greeted with silence. In all candidness, Scott believes he "failed miserably" to increase the Forum's membership base by drawing African Americans into the Forum.

While initial attempts to integrate the Forum may have failed, all was not lost. Both Forum presidents J. Hume Taylor, Jr., and Morton H. Clark continued the Forum's efforts to recruit African American members. As did Scott, they focused on Norfolk State University and also sought out faculty and administrators from Hampton University. In an interview, Clark stated he believes the Forum's efforts were rewarded when the first African American members joined the Forum during his presidency (1974-1975).

A number of prominent African Americans have addressed the forum, including William Raspberry (left), Carl Rowan (below), and Clarence Page (facing page). Photographs courtesy of Washington Speakers Bureau.

African American speakers also began to grace the Forum's stage. In what can only be described as an almost clairvoyant choice, the Forum chose as one of its speakers a man whose name would not be a household word for another five years. Alexander Palmer Murray Haley, better known as Alex Haley, who as a coast guardsman was stationed in Hampton Roads, returned to Norfolk on November 30, 1971. He appeared at the Forum while in the process of writing *Roots*. One Forum member remembers Haley recounting tales of the seven generations of his ancestors, including Kunta Kinte. However *Roots* would not be published until 1976.

Following Haley was *Washington Post* Pulitzer Prize columnist William J. Raspberry, who focused his January 18, 1977, talk on the decline of the American family. He argued that a number of outside influences, including economics, changing times, changing family structures, and psychological pressures, were weakening the traditional makeup of American families. Solutions offered by Raspberry included welfare reform, equality within the family structure, and "true intimate interaction" between parents and their children.

Other African Americans who have addressed the Forum included human rights activist Coretta Scott King (February 23, 1982), former Ambassador Carl Rowan (February 16, 1987), entertainer Pearl Bailey (October 20, 1987), musician Bobby Short (March 13, 1990), columnist Clarence Page (February 11, 1992), and General Colin Powell (September 20, 1994).

The Forum's efforts to bring African Americans into its roles preceded another Forum first, which took place in 1980. While women had long been involved with the operation of the Forum, serving on the board of directors, as secretaries, and as vice-presidents, none had served as its president. That changed when, in 1980, Betsy Trundle was elected to that office.

Born in Norfolk, Trundle graduated from Sweet Briar College and went on to work at the New York communications firm of Phil Dean Associates, rising to vice-president before departing to raise her family. She did not slow down, however. During her professional sabbatical, Trundle published two books, established the regional magazine *Port Folio*, and co-founded the d'Art Center in Norfolk.

Trundle had been active in the Forum for a number of years preceding her election to the presidency. For the October 14, 1969, appearance of Betty Furness, a champion of American consumers and former assistant to President Lyndon B. Johnson on consumer affairs, Trundle organized bus service for Forum members living in Virginia Beach. According to the *Pilot*, thirty-five passengers were required for the service to be used. The bus would depart Linkhorn Park School at 7 p.m. and make a stop at Princess Anne

High School shortly thereafter. Glenn Scott recalled the bus service on this occasion but is uncertain whether the service ran regularly.

While the complexion of the Forum's members and officers changed, the quality and timeliness of its speakers did not. There was, however, as noted previously, a shift to less serious topics. Former politicos contributed their share of lectures, but the number of scientists appearing before the Forum declined. The number of entertainers (in the broadest sense of the term) appearing before the Forum increased. But whether a former presidential aide, an author, a musician, a comedian, a sculptor, or a future Nobel Peace Prize winner, the lecturers were intriguing.

Well known print journalists such as Hanson Baldwin, Marquis W. Childs, and Harrison Salisbury continued to receive invitations to address the Forum. In addition, a new breed of journalist, the television journalist, began appearing. Daniel Schorr, Columbia Broadcasting System (CBS) news correspondent, appears to have been the first. Speaking January 7, 1964, Schorr's topic, "Behind the Scenes at East-West Crisis," focused on the Cuban Missile Crisis and its aftermath. Calling the tense days of October 1962 the "last great confrontation" between East and West, Schorr believed that the relationship between the two superpowers—the United States and the Soviet Union—had fundamentally been altered by the threat of nuclear war. Schorr addressed the Forum for a second time ten years later, on March 12, 1974.

Robert Pierpoint, CBS White House correspondent, also spoke to the Forum twice. On January 27, 1970, Pierpoint's lecture was entitled "View from the White House Steps." Pierpoint went on to become CBS diplomatic correspondent, and his lecture on October 12, 1982, dealt with the current state of United States foreign policy.

As other network news programs attempted to match the stature of CBS, their reporters also went on the lecture circuit. Harry Reasoner became the first non-CBS television correspondent to address the Forum. Speaking on October 15, 1974, Reasoner reviewed the nation's problems of the 1960s and early 1970s—assassinations, riots, Watergate, the resignation of Richard M. Nixon—and posed the question "Can we survive the '70s?" Reasoner then pointed to several bright spots: the decline in the country's birth rate, the wealth of land the United States has, and the country's middle class, whom he viewed as "the nation's hope for a bright future."

Diplomats, politicians, and other government officials have long been a part of the Forum's programs. However, during the 1960s, only four individuals attached to the United States government or the government of a foreign land addressed the Forum. Dr. Arthur Larson, author of *A Republican Looks at His Party*, former head of the United States Information Agency, and special consultant to President Dwight D. Eisenhower, spoke to the Forum on October 18, 1960. Larson's lecture that night focused on the failure of the United States to accurately and convincingly portray who Americans are in the nation's battle against Communism. This, Larson contended, was a result of putting the efforts of the United States into the negative side of being against Communism, rather than the positive example of who we are. Calling the current relationship between government, business, and workers in the United States "enterprise democracy," Larson argued that the three were not inherently antagonistic to each other but "support(ed) and advance(d) each other's interest." Not until March 1964, would the Forum host another politician.

With the continuing arms and space races, the early 1960s saw two scientists address the Forum. Willy Ley, appearing before the Forum on March 23, 1960, believed the United States was at least two-and-a-half years behind the Soviet Union in rocket technology. Praising the National Aeronautics and Space Administration for the strides it had made, Ley still predicted that the Soviet Union would achieve a "soft landing" on the moon before the United States. Perhaps naively, Ley did not believe that the two nations were involved in a race to develop rockets to deliver nuclear warheads, but rather they were in a "weight lifting" contest to see which country could develop the most lifting capabilities with their rockets.

A somber President John F. Kennedy spoke to the American people on the evening of October 22, 1962. Kennedy, as a result of the Soviet Union placing offensive missiles in Cuba, informed the country and the world that he had ordered a naval blockade of the island nation. The front page headline for the *Virginian-Pilot* the following day read: "Cuban Blockade Ordered: Stop or Be Sunk Red Ships Warned." An editorial on the growing crisis published on October 22, 1962, quoted from Dr. Ralph E. Lapp's book, *Kill and Overkill*, released that same day, stated that America should limit its output of nuclear weapons.

Dr. Ralph E. Lapp, nuclear physicist, in perhaps the best timed Forum appearance, addressed the Forum on October 23, 1962. Lapp blamed the late discovery of the offensive weapons in Cuba on poor spying by the United States. During the question-and-answer period, Lapp said he saw no practical use of nuclear weapons being launched from space because the current inter-continental missiles had numerous advantages. Lapp concluded, according to the *Pilot* "the future is 'a world of science, a new and revolutionary age.'"

Norfolk was not untouched by the crisis. Ships sailed from and to Norfolk, and over the next several days thousands of civilian refugees from the United States Naval Base, Guantanamo Bay, Cuba, arrived in Norfolk by ship. On Sunday, October 28, 1962, the Soviet Union agreed to dismantle and withdraw their missiles, ending the threat of a nuclear war.

While the Forum's past topics had been consistently serious in nature, there was a noticeable shift to more lighthearted fare during this peri-od. Actors, comedians, musicians, and others now took center stage. Satirists Malcolm Muggeridge and Russell Baker, and comedians Ray Middleton, Tom Ewell, Art Buchwald, and Mark Russell, all came to the Forum. Actors Thomas Mitchell, Vincent Price, Celeste Holm, Ray Bolger, Tom Poston, and musicians Meredith Wilson, Patrice Munsel, and Peter Duchin shared their thoughts on the arts with the Forum's audience. The Forum brought Baroness Von Trapp to Norfolk on November 24, 1964. The reality of the Von Trapp's escape from the Nazis must have been radically different from the happy-go-lucky, sing-along versions depicted on stage and screen.

After a four-year gap in politician-speakers, former Ecuadorian Minister of Foreign Affairs Dr. Jose Chiriboga addressed the Forum on March 24, 1964. Chiriboga touched on a number of topics, including the late President John F. Kennedy's Alliance for Progress, land reform, Latin America's commitment to democracy, and the economic status of Latin America. Chiriboga believed the alliance had already produced beneficial results in the three years the program had been in operation, and believed that over the next twenty years the alliance would benefit both Latin America and the United States.

Dr. Henry A. Kissinger, Harvard University professor of government, came to Norfolk in February 1966 to address the Forum. The former advisor to Henry Cabot Lodge, ambassador to South Vietnam, spoke of the ongoing war in Southeast Asia. From the newspaper account of his lecture, according to Kissinger, "the U.S. will not be defeated in the field." "The real problem," he continued, "is a political problem. Vietnam is a society but not a nation. It is a people but not a state." So the question he posed was how does the United States win a just and lasting peace? It was a question that would remain unanswered for another eight years, and whose answer remains in debate to this day.

A number of other politicians addressed the Forum in the early 1970s. Lord Harlech, who as Sir David Ormsby-Gore was the British Ambassador to the United States (1961-1965), spoke in October 1967 of the dangers of excessive nationalism. Roger Hilsman, a former assistant secretary of state for Far Eastern affairs, came to the Forum's stage in March 1971. Hilsman, who had resigned his position in the State Department as a protest to President Lyndon B. Johnson's continued escalation of the war in Vietnam, argued that the "Vietnamization" of the war would only prolong the fighting. Hilsman believed the war was a result, not of Communistic expansion, but rather of a "much deeper antagonism toward colonialism and as part of the world wide wave of nationalism."

Political issues held sway as the Forum's topic choice between the mid-1970s and 1980s. Speakers included Samuel Dash, chief counsel for the Senate Watergate Committee; Hugh Scott, republican leader in the Senate; John V. Lindsay, former mayor of New York City; Daniel Patrick Monynihan, senator-elect; Abba Eban, former Israeli Foreign Minister; Ramsey Clark, former attorney general of the United States; William Colby, former head of the Central Intelligence Agency; William Sullivan, former ambassador to Iran; Senators William Proxmire and Sam Ervin; former Presidential Press Secretary Jody Powell; Secretary of the Army John O. Marsh, Jr.; and finally, William H. Webster, director of the Federal Bureau of Investigation, addressed the Forum.

This twenty-plus-year period of the Forum's existence saw dramatic changes, both good and bad. Interest in the Forum, as judged by the Forum's ability to sell all its tickets prior to the opening of the season, appears to have waned. But even with all these changes, the Forum remained a functioning organization with its eye on the future, a future that grew brighter with each passing year, as we shall see.

British Prime Minister Margaret Thatcher spoke before the largest Norfolk
Forum audience ever on April 1, 1992. At left, Prime Minister Thatcher,
with the aid of Norfolk Forum President Monroe Kelly, III, takes questions
from the audience. Photograph courtesy of Monroe Kelly, III.

CHAPTER 6

RETURN TO GLORY

Having begun the process of righting itself during the mid-1980s, the Forum's return to prominence is nothing less than remarkable. For the 1984-1985 season, membership stood at 1,710, nearly one thousand subscribers below what Chrysler Hall could accommodate. Merely five years later, in 1990, the Forum, unable to meet the demand for tickets, had to return 480 requests, and created a waiting list of 100 individuals. In September 1991, and again in 1992, the Forum returned 1,500 subscription requests for their upcoming season. By the late 1990s, the Forum had been forced to limit its membership to approximately 3,000 and was consistently returning several hundred to several thousand season ticket requests per year.

As with the Forum's decline, what led to this remarkable turnaround cannot be precisely attributed to any single cause or person. Perhaps the single most important factor was the return to more traditional lectures, a step probably taken as a result of several member surveys. In the past, the Forum had conducted surveys to determine possible future speakers. J.E. Capps, Forum president at the time, had invited Forum subscribers' input back in 1938. Dorothy Thompson, who had previously spoken to the Forum on October 29 and 30, 1936, received the most votes for a return engagement. Eventually, Thompson did return, on February 7, 1956. Other potential lecturers mentioned, but who did not appear, included Alice Roosevelt Longworth, daughter of President Theodore Roosevelt; Winston Churchill, former prime minister of Great Britain and member of the British Parliament; Philip La Follette, governor of Wisconsin; and Thomas Mann, a German author who was in a self-imposed exile from his fatherland. While Philip La Follette did not appear before the Forum, his brother, Senator Robert M. La Follette, Jr., debated Representative Hamilton Fish on March 26, 1938. Erika Mann, Thomas

The distinguished jurist, and former judge of the U.S. District Court of Appeals of the District of Columbia, Robert Bork (second from right) joins fellow judges from Hampton Roads (left to right): Judge Robert G. Dumar, Judge Everett Martin, Jr., and Judge Lydia Calvert Taylor.

The Forum sometimes departs from its program of serious speakers. On September 29, 1992, President Monroe Kelly, III, introduced the Capitol Steps, who entertained the audience with a program of musical political satire. Photograph courtesy of Washington Speakers Bureau.

Mann's daughter, spoke on February 11, 1947. On a broader question as to general occupations or fields of expertise, Forum members requested ambassadors, European experts, explorers, and health experts, among others.

In 1986, the Forum again surveyed its membership. The survey, conducted by Forum Secretary Kathy Steadman, was distributed at the Forum's first lecture of the 1986-1987 season. The results of the survey were discussed at the June 1987, board of directors meeting. Unfortunately the minutes do not include a listing of the survey's results; however, it can be no small coincidence that, at this time when speaker selection shifted back to more serious topics, membership began its precipitous climb back to earlier sell-out crowds.

As in the past, journalists continued to dominate those selected to speak, but the political heavyweights returned, displacing the large number of entertainers of the previous years. Former Chief Justice Warren E. Burger became the only Supreme Court justice to address the Forum when he spoke on November 17, 1987. Burger, who was heading the Constitution Bicentennial Commission, entitled his lecture "We the People." He was followed by Thomas P. "Tip" O'Neill, Jr., former Speaker of the House; Zbigniew Brzezinski, President Jimmy Carter's National Security Advisor; and Dr. Henry A. Kissinger, Nobel Peace Prize recipient and Richard Nixon's Secretary of State.

While the Forum hosted only two former heads of state in its first fifty-five years, it has presented five in the last ten years, including Gerald Ford and George Bush (the only former United States presidents to address the Forum); former British Prime Ministers Margaret Thatcher and John Major (who joined early Forum speaker and British Prime Minister Clement Attlee); and Canadian Prime Minister Brian Mulroney.

Gerald Ford, following his introduction by G. William Whitehurst on September 20, 1989, spoke on a wide range of topics. He focused on the failure of the "war on drugs" to include alcoholism. On foreign affairs, Ford

Forum president Carter Grandy Scott poses with former Speaker of the House Thomas P. O'Neill, Jr., on April 17, 1990. O'Neill was only the second Speaker of the House to address the Forum. Photograph courtesy of Carter Grandy Scott.

cautioned that, when dealing with the Soviet Union, "we should continue to keep our guard up and our powder dry."

Former President George Bush appeared before the Norfolk Forum audience in what appears to have been a tentative step by the Forum to reach out to a larger audience. In honor of Presidents Day, February 21, 1994, the Forum had arranged for the special appearance of Bush when they learned that he might be available after they had already booked a schedule of speakers for that season. According to a February 5, 1994, article in the *Virginian-Pilot*, tickets were offered first to Forum subscribers; the 300 tickets left were then offered to non-subscribers and quickly sold out.

Margaret Thatcher spoke before the largest Norfolk Forum audience ever on April 1, 1992. In another venue experiment, the Forum moved the lecture from Chrysler Hall to Norfolk Scope, and the estimated audience of 6,000 heard Thatcher argue that NATO was as important now as it had been at the height of the Cold War. Thatcher also believed the West should not fear the breakup of the Soviet Union, but instead do all possible to help the fledgling republics. Five years

Ross Perot (right), businessman and presidential candidate, enjoys himself with members of the Norfolk Forum at a reception given in his honor. Joining him (left to right) are Marianne Matson, John P. Matson, Glenn Scott, and Carter Grandy Scott. Photograph courtesy of the Norfolk Forum.

Former Secretary of State and National Security Advisor, Dr. Henry A. Kissinger, is the only Nobel Peace Prize recipient to have addressed the Forum. Photograph by Bachrach; courtesy of Kissinger Associates.

later, on October 16, 1997, The Right Honorable John Major spoke of a bright future when addressing the Forum. Major predicted that the free market reforms taking root in the former Soviet Union and other third world countries would lift 50 percent of the world's poor countries out of poverty within a decade, "if governments can keep the peace."

In 1995, the Norfolk Forum conducted another survey of its members. This survey also focused on potential speakers and, of the 3,112 surveys mailed out, nearly one-third were returned. As with the 1938 survey, subscribers were requested to rank broad categories of expertise in order of desirability. Politics came in first, followed by media and journalism, authors, business and finance, history (in a surprisingly strong showing), entertainment, education, technical and scientific, and finally sports.

Forum leaders again were listening. A numbers of speakers recommended—for example, Mark Russell, Charlie Rose, and Barbara Walters—all appeared the following season. Former Senator Robert Dole appeared on November 11, 1997, and his wife Elizabeth Dole is the inaugural speaker for the 1998-1999 season.

One speaker's engagement is a testament to the tenacity of Forum leaders to get their chosen speaker. Considering the ranks of its speakers—news correspondents, diplomats, and high-ranking politicians—it is only natural that scheduled lecturers would have to withdraw at the last moment. The Forum's leadership, however, did not appreciate one speaker's attempt to cancel an appearance.

Only months before an announced and fully subscribed season, Forum President Jo Ann Hofheimer received word that a guest had decided to cancel not only the Forum appearance but all speaking engagements. Hofheimer presented ten possible alternative dates; each was rejected. The board of directors, with a sizable deposit and a contract signed six months previously, authorized a letter of objection to the speaker's agents. The letter cited the Forum's reputation of presenting quality lecturers "consistent with its promised program." The letter continued, "Never in more than 60 years of Forum history, has it ever been suggested to the Forum that a speaker has the right to simply trim back their commitments." The determination of the Forum's leadership had the desired result. Within a week the guest had confirmed the original date.

With attendance way up, Forum leadership turned its attention to another difficulty that had surfaced partly as a result of the dip in membership. The cost of engaging quality speakers for the Forum's programs escalated. The 1945-1946 season is the earliest year for which there is a complete expenditure report. The Forum paid a total of $1,050 for its five-speaker program that season, for which season tickets cost a mere $1.50. The cost for five speakers during the 1960-1961 program ran to $2,600. By then, season ticket prices had doubled, to $3.00. It appears to have remained at $3.00 until the 1966-1967 season when the cost of a season ticket went to $4.00. By 1983-1984, the Forum's budget for speakers had increased to $18,500, with a corresponding increase in season ticket cost: $15 for the 1983-1984 program.

Allan Donn, quoted in William Ruehlmann's October 30, 1983, *Virginian-Pilot* article, "Forum Still the Talk of the Town," noted that the Forum had never spent time fund-raising, but "the bad part is that we may

Senator John Warner (left) and President George Bush (center) are escorted by Forum President and Mrs. Thomas Shuttleworth. Photograph courtesy of Thomas Shuttleworth.

have to, now." His words proved painfully true when, in what appears to have been a first in the Forum's long history, a speaker was removed from the program as a result of a budget shortfall. Pulitzer Prize-winning author David McCullough's scheduled Forum appearance had to be postponed from the 1986-1987 season to the following year.

There are several explanations as to the drastically escalating cost of speakers during this period. First, the nation experienced double-digit inflation during the late 1970s, which naturally resulted in increased prices. Second, while speaker agencies had been used extensively to arrange speakers in the past, a number of lecturers had been brought to Norfolk through personal contact and charged the Forum only a nominal fee. Finally, former Forum President Glenn Scott stated in an interview that he believes the increase in speakers' fees was due, in part, to the nation's colleges. Colleges and universities developed public lecture programs subsidized in part by private donations and public monies (Old Dominion University's President's Lecture Series, for example), and therefore were able to offer higher fees to speakers in a very competitive field. Ruehlmann, at the end of his article, wondered if the Forum would survive. His conclusion: "Well, if folks keep buying tickets. And, now, if others will donate some funds to keep ticket prices thin . . .," then the Forum will be able to continue.

British Prime Minister Margaret Thatcher spoke before the largest Norfolk Forum audience ever on April 1, 1992. Thatcher portrait courtesy of Washington Speakers Bureau.

Folks kept buying tickets, but rather than wait for donations, the Forum sought ways to increase funding. Unlike many other lecture series, the Forum accepts no public subsidies, nor does it accept any corporate sponsorship of its lectures. In September 1990, President Carter Grandy Scott appointed Clifford Cutchins as chair, and Gary Rubin and Frederick Martin as members of a committee to consider, for apparently the first time, the question of establishing an endowment fund.

On May 16, 1991, Frederick Martin presented the Endowment Committee's report to the board. The committee determined that an endowment fund was not desirable or appropriate and stated it believed that any contributions or bequests to the Forum should be funneled through the Norfolk Foundation, a community fund managed by the city to fund specific causes. (It is not unusual for cities to have such foundations, where organizations combine their funds to maximize investments while still controlling the use of profits.) The Endowment Committee felt that using the Norfolk Foundation option would free the Forum from having to create a new business entity with the accompanying staffing and additional Internal Revenue Service reporting.

The Endowment Committee, on a motion by Judge Lydia Taylor, was then commissioned to explore creating a fund through the Norfolk Foundation, and Lee Kitchin, executive director of the Foundation, recalls at least one preliminary discussion between the Foundation and the Forum. Unfortunately, what transpired at this and any subsequent meetings between the Forum and the Foundation is unknown, and apparently the matter was not pursued beyond this stage.

The idea of an endowment fund, however, would not go away, and several times between 1991 and 1995, the board, through its committees, would address the question. Each time it was tabled for various reasons. These included a perceived restriction on surplus funds (which later proved inaccurate), and the reasoning from one committee that an endowment fund "for which there is no customer interest" was unwise. The establishment of a working relationship with the W.B. Shafer World Peace Trust to co-sponsor some lectures solved the endowment dilemma for the time being.

Bruce Shafer, born in Norfolk, Virginia, on October 22, 1894, worked most of his adult life in causes that would benefit mankind. Upon his death in September 1990, he funded the Bruce Shafer World Peace Trust, stipulating that funds were to be used in promoting world peace.

A portion of a letter, believed to be from Forum President Thomas Shuttleworth to the board of directors, provides the first evidence of a possible relationship between the two organizations. Gordon Tayloe, trustee of the Trust, contacted Shuttleworth with a proposal that the Trust once a year co-sponsor a speaker "of worldwide importance" on the broadly defined subject of world peace. The Trust proposed a $15,000 annual donation for such a speaker, an amount that would increase by 5 percent yearly. Speaker selection, Shuttleworth assured Forum directors, would remain in the "relatively unfettered province of the Speaker Committee of the Forum."

Even before a formal agreement was signed, perhaps as a sign of good faith, the Trust contributed some $16,400 to the Forum in early 1994, with the understanding that, if the agreement was reached, the money would be returned. On January 19, 1995, the Norfolk Forum agreed to "create as one of its annual lectures series the 'W.B. Shafer World Peace Lecture,'" with selection of the speaker left to the Forum. The Trust could, however, disapprove of its donation being used on a speaker that it did not feel met its criteria. There is no provision in the agreement that requires the Forum to return unused monies. Upon execution of the agreement, the Trust forward-

On September 19, 1995, Brian Mulroney, former Prime Minister of Canada, became the sixth head of state to address the Forum. Photograph courtesy of Washington Speakers Bureau.

ed an additional $16,000 to the Forum, bringing the donations to over $32,000.

On September 19, 1995, former Canadian Prime Minister Brian Mulroney became the first of three lecturers to be co-sponsored by an agency outside the Forum. The other two speakers co-sponsored by the Trust have been Jane Goodall on April 1, 1997, and former British Prime Minister John Major on October 15, 1997.

Even with additional funding, the Forum still faced the problem of expansion. Moving the Forum to the Norfolk Scope on a permanent basis was discussed. However, because of the acoustics, there was little support for this option despite the success of Margaret Thatcher's appearance at Scope April 1, 1992. Instead, the Forum decided that same month to explore alternative formats that would increase the Forum's membership base. The Planning Committee was charged with focusing on "any ways and means of accommodating the substantial demand we have for subscriptions we can not supply."

Jane Goodall (center) was one of three lecturers co-sponsored by the W.B. Shafer World Peace Trust. Pictured with Goodall are Forum president Jo Ann Hofheimer and John H. Tucker, Jr., Forum president 1987-1988. Photograph courtesy John H. Tucker, Jr.

The first alternative considered was presenting the speakers at two lectures. The directors may not have been aware that this format had been used during the 1935-1936 season and for three of the five lectures during 1936-1937. However, considering the current fee for lecturers, the additional staff required, and the difficulty of booking a speaker for two consecutive nights, this proposal was tabled.

At the May 1992 directors meeting, Roy Martin raised the possibility of the Forum conducting two separate lectures series, "an A and B series," as he called it. Considering

this and other options, the Planning Committee reported its findings to the directors in September 1992. They believed there were two issues confronting the Forum: first, what would be the maximum amount to pay for any given speaker (an issue the committee felt was outside its purview); and secondly, how would the Forum handle the increased demand for tickets. (In 1992, the Forum received roughly 6,000 requests for its approximately 3,000 tickets.)

The committee proposed two options to deal with the latter predicament. It recommended exploring the possibility of creating a second Forum lecture series. Both series would consist of four speakers each, with one of the four speakers being held in common between both series. This common lecture would be presented at a combined meeting held at the Norfolk Scope. The remaining three lectures for each series (a total of six) would be presented separately at Chrysler Hall. There would be no single ticket sales, in keeping with the general tradition of the Forum.

A second option proposed by the committee was to create a Virginia Beach Forum operated by the Norfolk Forum. Unable to reach a decision on which option to pursue, the board returned the problem to both the Planning and the Program committees for further investigation. The lively debate regarding a second series continued for several years. At one point, the Program and Planning committees met in joint session in October 1991, and the directors discussed their combined report on December 2, 1991. Members of the Program Committee did not feel a second series was a viable alternative, while members of the Planning Committee believed a second series would succeed. Both Roy Martin and L.D. Britt favored this second series, but a majority of directors held severe reservations that a second series would pose a financial risk the Forum was not prepared to take.

About this same time, the board explored television as a means to expand. The use of closed-circuit television had first been brought before the board in 1989 and, by 1992, sites such as the Marriott Hotel, Chrysler Hall's rehearsal hall, and the Wells Theater were being considered as possible satellite locations. In addition, although initial contacts between the Forum and Old Dominion University's Academic Television Services and public broadcasting affiliate WHRO seemed encouraging, the question of who retained rights became insurmountable. Finally, in a move to test the interest in closed-circuit broadcasting, the directors conducted a survey of individuals who had not received season tickets. Of five hundred surveys mailed, only

Facing page: John Major (center), former British Prime Minister, is the seventh head of state to address the Forum. Pictured with him at a reception in his honor are William R. Van Buren, III, and Norfolk Mayor Paul Fraim. 1997 photograph courtesy of Anthony Mauer.

Dr. L.D. Britt, the Forum's current first vice-president will become the first African American president following the term of William R. Van Buren, III. Photograph courtesy of Dr. L.D. Britt.

fifty-six were returned and, of those, only thirty-seven wished to view the lectures via a closed-circuit hookup. The directors interpreted the low return as an indication there was not enough interest and dismissed this option as well.

Part of the motivation to establish a second Forum in Virginia Beach was to head off any potential rival. But competition had not been seen as a threat in the early days. Founder Dr. Vincent H. Ober, in 1935, chaired the Norfolk Kiwanis Club's Great Adventure Lecture Series. In the late 1930s, Forum members and founders, the Reverend C.M. Gordon, Rabbi Mendoza and Cherry Nottingham, assisted in the formation of the Norfolk Town Meetings. Another former member, Mrs. A.O. Calcott, served as an officer of the Portsmouth Forum.

Even outside board meetings, the debate between Forum members is lively, such as this obviously light-hearted exchange between former Norfolk Mayor Joseph Leafe and Forum Director Carter Grandy Scott. Photograph courtesy of the Norfolk Forum.

But unlike those early leaders, the current Norfolk Forum leadership believed the creation of any new forums would be harmful. The Junior League of Norfolk and Virginia Beach planned a lecture series opening in 1991. In May 1990, Forum directors authorized a letter to the League noting the Norfolk Forum's concerns that this new forum would be in direct competition. Carter Grandy Scott informed Forum directors in September that the League did not plan to duplicate the Forum and would focus on issues of concern to the League, such as child abuse.

But this fear of competition continued to plague the directors, perhaps with good reason. Already the Tidewater Jewish Forum had kicked off its own successful speaker series. In 1991-1992, according to the May 22, 1991, *Virginian-Pilot*, the Tidewater Jewish Forum would feature such diverse speakers as comedienne Joan Rivers, former *New York Times* Executive Editor A.M. Rosenthal, novelist Leon Uris, and actress Tovah Feldshuh. And both the Portsmouth Forum and Old Dominion University's President's Lecture Series were doing well.

Roy Martin, in April 1992, suggested the Forum may be opening the gates for another organization to start a rival speakers' series "if the Norfolk Forum did not expand in some manner." His words would prove prophetic.

In 1994, the Planning Committee returned to the feasibility of establishing a separate Virginia Beach Forum operated by the Norfolk Forum. To reduce competition between the two circuits, the Virginia Beach lectures would be held during the spring and summer months. Once again the debate was wide-ranging and lively, covering both the positive and negative effects a new series might have on the Norfolk series. Still the Forum's directors backed away, deciding not to extend itself financially on a second lecture series in Virginia Beach. Instead it suggested yet another look at an endowment, this time to cover the startup cost of a new series in the future, and a re-examination of the second series in two to three years.

They never got the chance. On Sunday, January 7, 1996, the Virginia Beach *Beacon* announced the debut of the Virginia Beach Forum. Ironically, its first speaker, on February 9, would be Cable News Network talk show host Larry King. King had been featured at the Norfolk Forum that same month exactly ten years before. All 1,100 seats in the Pavilion were sold out for King's appearance at the Beach.

The article announcing the Beach Forum quoted founder Kathy Katsias as stating that it did not plan to compete with the Norfolk Forum. "'I've been a member of the (Norfolk) Forum for many years,' she explained. 'It's always a rush to get your money in for the following year or you don't get tickets. Since tickets are not readily available to the Norfolk Forum,' she went on, 'it's time to give an alternative.'"

The Virginia Beach Forum may have duplicated speakers but apparently did not plan to follow the Norfolk Forum's other practices. According to the *Beacon*, it hoped to offer sponsorships, as well as "a range of public personalities such as athletes, mystery writers and even musical groups." Like the Norfolk Forum, the Virginia Beach series is limited by the 1,000-plus seats in the Pavilion. But, unlike the Forum, Katsias stated they were prepared to consider an unusual venue such as the Virginia Beach amphitheater.

Has competition harmed the Forum? It may be too soon to tell, but if the numbers speak for themselves, consider this: Once again, for its 1998-1999 season, Norfolk Forum season tickets are sold out and a large number of potential subscribers had to be turned down. Maybe the lesson lies in the words of Ken Burns who addressed the Norfolk Forum's sold-out crowd on February 27, 1996, when he described America: "It was made up as people went along," much the same as the Forum. Another analogy may lie in the words of Cokie Roberts, also a 1996 speaker, who stated in an interview describing the panel joining her on the ABC Sunday morning news program: "All of us on the panel like and respect each other." This also seems the case historically with directors of the Forum.

In a January 1, 1997, article in the *Virginian-Pilot* which referred to the Norfolk Forum, columnist Guy Friddell quoted F. Scott Fitzgerald as stating, "the test of a first rate intelligence 'is the ability to hold two opposed ideas in mind at the same time and still retain the ability to function.'"

Monroe Kelly, III (left), Marian Shuttleworth and Dr. John F. Stecker, Jr., enjoy a moment at one of the many receptions to welcome Forum speakers. Photograph courtesy of the Norfolk Forum.

The final evening of the Forum's 1997-1998 season boasted columnist Dave Barry for yet another sold-out crowd. Barry is pictured here with Forum Treasurer Richard G. Diamonstein. 1998 photograph courtesy of Anthony Mauer.

Perhaps the Forum had been following the same credo as Forum lecturer Jane Goodall, who told the Forum audience April 1, 1997, "what's most important is not how we got the way we are, but who we are today. . .. I've seen ordinary people tackle problems in extraordinary ways." Finally, when Bob Dole addressed yet another sold-out crowd November 11, 1997, he named Dwight D. Eisenhower as his "idol." He continued, "I think Eisenhower's strength came from an internal compass, an integrity that emerged from his core and elevated those around him." All of these qualities would also seem to apply to the Forum visionaries.

In its 65 years, the leaders of the Norfolk Forum—from Dr. Vincent H. Ober and Cherry Nottingham through the decades to today's Forum leadership—have demonstrated a faith that knowledge is power, that an informed citizenry is democracy's greatest strength and asset. What has endured is the same faith that NBC News anchorman Tom Brokaw declared in his January 24, 1993, Norfolk Forum address: "that there is a place for everyone in the spectrum . . .. And the American people have a pretty good record of sorting out what counts and what doesn't."

In its 65 years, the leaders of the Norfolk Forum have demonstrated a faith that knowledge is power, that an informed citizenry is democracy's greatest strength and asset.

Since its founding, the torch of Forum leadership has passed to countless other hands. Sadly, the person who was perhaps most influential in the Forum's founding, Dr. Vincent H. Ober, died on October 21, 1994, more than 62 years after that first delegation of citizens met at the Monticello Hotel to explore the possibility of a public speaking forum. In its 65 years of providing this service, the Forum's leadership has elected to steer a steady course. It is a course that has served the Forum well. Other lecture series have come and gone, but the Norfolk Forum endures. It is the granddaddy of them all, and it is arguably "the best ticket in town."

THE NORFOLK FORUM

A Nonprofit Community Organization Founded in 1933

LECTURE SERIES
1998-1999

The Board of Directors of the Norfolk Forum is pleased to announce the 1998-1999 season. Programs will be held at Chrysler Hall at 8:15 p.m. on the dates indicated. In order to provide the broadest community participation, subscribers may only purchase the number of tickets that the subscriber purchased last season. Tickets are available **only** for the entire series; no tickets are available for individual lectures. The series price will be $70.00. Programs have sold out quickly in the past, so we urge you to subscribe right away. We look forward to what promises to be one of our most exciting seasons. Please join us for what we trust will be another memorable forum series.

William R. Van Buren, III
President
Program Committee
Chairman

ELIZABETH DOLE

ELIZABETH DOLE
President of the American Red Cross, Secretary of Transportation under Ronald Reagan and Secretary of Labor under George Bush, Elizabeth Dole was recently counted among the top ten most admired women in the world. Learn of her perspective on world and domestic affairs as she shares with our audience her future agenda.

Thursday, October 1, 1998 — 8:15 p.m.

DAN RATHER

DAN RATHER
As anchor of the CBS Evening News, Dan Rather has had a front row seat on world history. Far from a passive observer, he has personally reported from the scene in Vietnam, Afghanistan, the Persian Gulf and Bosnia. His watchword is integrity, a theme that may be too lightly heralded in an age of media sensationalism.

Sunday, November 8, 1998 — 8:15 p.m.

GARY TRUDEAU

GARY TRUDEAU
Never interviewed and seldom available on the lecture circuit, Gary Trudeau has remained visible only through the characters of his daily political cartoon, *Doonesbury*. Armed with a keen and insightful humor, he will deliver a light and humorous reflection on his career and the political absurdities so deftly captured by his cartoon sketches.

Tuesday, February 23, 1999 — 8:15 p.m.

DAVID BRESHEARS

DAVID BRESHEARS
Clients pay as much as $65,000 to scale the heights of Mount Everest, the highest point on earth. For the mere price of a Norfolk Forum ticket, David Breshears will take you there with brilliant images and vivid tales of his fourth ascent. Producer of the IMAX film, *Everest*, which debuted in March, 1998, David Breshears led a team of film makers on an impossible mission and succeeded despite terrible odds and the daunting vision of the bodies of nine climbers who died on the mountain as his team prepared for their ascent.

Tuesday, May 11, 1999 — 8:15 p.m.

A Forward Look

Like the rivers that wash the shores of Hampton Roads, the free flow of ideas disseminated by Norfolk Forum programs has connected us all to the communities beyond the narrow confines of our own borders. Its speakers have raised our consciousness of complicated world issues, expanded our understanding of the political landscape that is so often superficially treated in mass media, and taken our thoughts to places and events which reside only in our imagination.

Free from the influence of any political cause, corporate constituency or special interest group, the Norfolk Forum has relied on the sole support of its loyal subscribers and its faithful individual volunteers to advance its mission of enlightening and entertaining the citizens of Hampton Roads. Daniel J. Boorstin, former Librarian of Congress and a Forum speaker in 1974, stated in the July 12, 1998, *Parade*: "Democracy has no orthodoxy, but it can survive and flourish only with a literate citizenry." The founders of the Norfolk Forum knew the value of an informed citizenry and the benefit of fresh thought and insightful discussion coursing through the veins of a community. Those founders shared a common conviction that citizens who endeavored to deeply understand the complex issues of our society were far better participants in the democratic process. To those founders, we are deeply grateful for their foresight. To our audience, we are pleased that so many share our love of politics, adventure and entertainment.

Your leadership is committed to the legacy that is the Norfolk Forum—where the world's leading figures are brought to the doorstep of Hampton Roads, connecting us to the political and social fabric of the world around us much as our harbors link us to the lifelines of world commerce. We hope you have enjoyed our memories of the Forum's past and that you will continue to share with us its bright future. The commitment of our leadership to deliver to our audience the best and most provocative speakers of our time is unwavering and promises that a Norfolk Forum ticket will remain the "best ticket in town."

William R. Van Buren, III
President, Norfolk Forum

The current Norfolk Forum leadership is (seated, left to right) President William Van Buren, III, and First Vice-President Dr. L. D. Britt; (standing, left to right) Second Vice-President William W. "Will" King, Secretary Alice Mountjoy, and Treasurer Richard G. Diamonstein. Photograph courtesy of the Norfolk Forum.

Facing page: Once again, the Forum's 1998-1999 season sets the standard for quality speakers, as one can see from the coming lineup. Flyer courtesy of the Norfolk Forum.

Norfolk Forum Speakers*

Season-Date	Speaker Occupation
1933-1934	
October 30	Henry T. Rainey, Speaker of the House
January 22	Upton Close, Writer
February 27	Max Forrester Eastman, Poet; Editor
March 28	Henry J. Allen, Former Senator
1934-1935	
November 27	Ruth Bryan Owen, Ambassador to Denmark
January 24	Dr. Robert E. Hutchens, President, University of Chicago
February 19	Dr. S. Parkes Cadman, Clergy
March 14	Dr. Will Durant, Philosopher
1935-1936	
October 29 & 30	Dorothy Thompson, Journalist
December 10 & 11	S. Miles Bouton, Correspondent
January 13 & 14	William Beebe, Scientist
February 10 & 11	George Sokolsky, Journalist
March 30 & 31	J. Fred Essary, Correspondent
1936-1937	
October 19 & 20	Cosmo Hamilton, Playwright
November 30 & December 1	Dr. Irving Fisher, Professor of Economics
January 18	Alben William Barkley, Senator
February 16	George Fort Milton, Editor, *Chattanooga News*
March 15 & 16	Dr. Lewis Berg, Psychologist
1937-1938	
October 12	Dr. Henry C. McComas, Psychologist
November 16	Dr. E.W. Kemmerer, Professor of Economics
January 6	Dr. Will Durant, Philosopher; Pulitzer Prize
March 26	Robert M. LaFollete, Jr., Senator & Hamilton Fish, Representative
1938-1939	
November 23	Dr. No-yung Park, Chinese & Dr. Yutaka Minakuchi, Japanese
January 23	Dr. Pitrim Sorokin, Early Russian revolutionary
February 21	Maurice Hindus, Author
March 30	Isaac F. Morrisson, Interviewer

Season-Date	Speaker Occupation
1939-1940	
October 3	Vincent Sheean, Author
November 8	Herbert Agar, Assoc. Editor, *Louisville Courier-Journal*; Pulitzer Prize
January 8	Alfred Duff Cooper, English statesman
March 8	Stringfellow Barr, Pres., St. John's College; Rhodes Scholar
1940-1941	
October 30	Channing Pollock, Author; Playwright
February 19	Dr. William Starr Myers, Professor of politics
1941-1942	
November 8	Anne O'Hare McCormick, Foreign correspondent; Pulitzer Prize
December 2	Henry C. Wolfe, Foreign affairs expert
January 9	Dr. Ricardo Alfaro, Former president, Republic of Panama
February 11	Jay Allen, Correspondent
1942-1943	
November 13	Louis Fischer, Journalist; Author
December 9	Walter Duranty, Correspondent; Pulitzer Prize
January 7	Hallett Abend, Correspondent
February 11	Dorothy Crawford, Dramatic star
March [?]	James R. Young, Dir., International Service Bureau in the Orient
1943-1944	
October 26	John Goette, Foreign correspondent
November [?]	Wallace R. Devel
January 12	Ray Brock, Correspondent
March 8	Andre Micholopoulos, Former Greek Minister of Information
March 26	Carlos P. Romulo, Diplomat; Pulitzer Prize
1944-1945	
November 21	T.A. Raman, Head, India Information Service
December 12	Ray Josephs, Correspondent
January 16	Beardsley Ruml, Author; Economist
February 26	H.H. Knickerbocker, Journalist; Pulitzer Prize
April 18	Maurice Hindus, Correspondent
1945-1946	
October 11	Vincent Sheean, War correspondent
November 11	Max Hill
January 15	William Lydgate, Chief editor, Gallup Poll
February 20	Dr. H. H. Chang, Chinese statesman
April 16	Douglas Miller, Economist

*Based on records available.

1946-1947

October 8	Dr. Gerald Wendt, Science editor
November 19	Dr. James M. Hepbron, Criminologist
January 7	Stuart Chase, Economist
February 11	Erika Mann, Daughter of Thomas Mann
March 18	Nicol Smith, Spy

1947-1948

October 13	Rear Admiral E. M. Zacharias (Ret), U.S. Navy Intelligence
January 6	Marquis W. Childs, Columnist; Pulitzer Prize
February 10	Dr. Douglas M. Kelly, Prof., Bowman Gray School of Med., Wake Forest College
February 24	Leigh White, Foreign correspondent
March 15	James Warner Bellah, Author
April 6	Herbert Agar, Editor, *Louisville Courier-Journal*; Pulitzer Prize

1948-1949

October 26	Cod Meyer, Jr., Pres., United World Federalists
December 8	Dr. Morris Fishbein, Medical Doctor
February 1	Robert Magidoff, Journalist
February 28	John W. Vandercook, Radio commentator; Author

1949-1950

November 7	Hanson W. Balwin, Military editor, *New York Times*; Pulitzer Prize
December 6	Frank P. Graham, Senator
January 19	Dr. David Bradley, Scientist
February 28	Dr. Quincy Howe, Author; Editor
April 11	Leverett Saltonstall, Senator

1950-1951

October 26	Adm. Louis E. Denfeld, Former Chief of Naval Operations
December 5	Alexander Gabriel, Commentator on the U.N.
January 10	Mrs. Vera Micheles Dean, Dir., Research Dept., Foreign Policy Association
February 19	Harrison Forman, Expert on Far East
March 27	Donald F. Richberg, Former asst. to Franklin D. Roosevelt

1951-1952

November 5	Dr. Will Durant, Philosopher; Pulitzer Prize
December 4	Herbert L. Matthews, Journalist
January 22	Mrs. Ruth Bryan Owen, Former congresswoman; U.S. Minister to Denmark
March 5	George V. Denny, Jr., Founder & Moderator, *America's Town Meeting of the Air*
April 8	John Temple Graves, Alabama editor; Lecturer & Dr. Kurt Singer, Radio commentator; Author

1952-1953

October 28	Hugh D. Scott, Jr., Representative & Brook Hays, Representative
December 9	Werner Knop, Diplomat
February 24	Doris Fleeson, Correspondent
April 8	Herbert Philbrick, Former domestic counterespionage agent

1953-1954

October 21	Lady Rama Rau, Wife of Sir Benegal Rau, former Indian ambass. to U.S.
November 17	Walter Crawford Kelly, Creator, *Pogo*
January 20	Colgate W. Darden, Jr., Former governor of Va.; President, University of Va.
February 25	Edward A. Weeks, Editor, *Atlantic Monthly*

1954-1955

October 20	John Dos Passos, Social historian; Novelist
November 24	Roscoe Drummond, Columnist
February 22	Ogden Nash, Poet
March 29	Dr. Ralph E. Lapp, Dir., Nuclear Science Service

1955-1956

October 25	Judge Harold R. Medina, U.S. Circuit Court of Appeals, N.Y.
January 17	Eddy Gilmore, Journalist; Pulitzer Prize
February 7	Dorothy Thompson, Columnist
March 6	Robert Shaw, Radio; TV writer

1956-1957

October 2	Herbert Morrison, Former Deputy Prime Minister, Great Britain
January 8	Dr. I. M. Levitt, Astronomer
February 19	Stewart Alsop, Journalist
March 13	Dr. Marion Mill Preminger, Socialite

1957-1958

October 1	Dr. Will Durant, Philosopher, Pulitzer Prize
November 19	Helen & Frank Schreider, Adventurers
January 21	Agna Enters, Dance mime; Painter; Sculptor
February 25	Hanson Baldwin, Journalist; Military analyst

1958-1959

October 28	Edward Weeks, Editor, *Atlantic Monthly*
December 9	Anthony Nutting, Member, British Parliament
January 20	Carlos P. Romulo, Former Philippine ambassador to U.S.
February 24	Harrison Evans Salisbury, Columnist; Pulitzer Prize

1959-1960

October 14	Vijaya L. Pandit, Sister of Indian Prime Minister Nehru
December 1	Louis Untermeyer, Poet; Anthologist
February 8	Earl Clement Attlee, Former Prime Minister, Great Britain
March 22	Willy Ley, Authority on space travel

1960-1961

October 18	Dr. Arthur Larson, Head, U.S. Information Agency; Author
November 15	Marquis W. Childs, Journalist
January 24	Fiore de Henriques, Sculptor
February 28	William L. Shirer, Correspondent
April 18	Brig. Gen. Robert L. Scott (Ret.), Pilot, USAF

1961-1962

October 31	Thomas Mitchell, Actor
November 21	Vance Packard, Social analyst
January 16	William H. Stringer, Journalist
February 13	Edgar Snow, China authority
March 13	Willem L. Oltmans, Dutch correspondent

1962-1963
October 23   Dr. Ralph E. Lapp, Space-age scientist
November 20   Malcolm Muggeridge, Satirist
January 15   Lisa Howard, Correspondent; Author
February 12   Richard L. Tobin, Editor, *Saturday Review of Literature*
March 14   Vincent Price, Actor; Art connoisseur

1963-1964
October 29   Allen Drury, Political novelist; Pulitzer Prize
November 21   Ray Middleton, Comedian
January 7   Daniel Schorr, Correspondent
February 18   Harrison Evans Salisbury, Journalist; Pulitzer Prize
March 24   Dr. Jose R. Chiriboga, Diplomat

1964-1965
October 27   Kenneth G. Crawford, Correspondent
November 24   Baroness Von Trapp
January 12   Richard C. Hottelet, Commentator
February 23   Authur Schlesinger, Jr., Special Assistant to John F. Kennedy

1965-1966
October 5   Dr. A. L. Rowse, Elizabethan-age expert
November 9   Leon Volkov, Journalist, *Newsweek*
January 18   Stringfellow Barr, Historian; Former pres., St. John's College
February 15   Dr. Henry A. Kissinger, Professor of government, Harvard University
March 15   Tom Ewell, Comedian

1966-1967
October 18   Drew Middleton, Journalist
November 22   Art Buchwald, Humorist
February 14   Han Suyin, Author
April 4   Jim Fowler, Naturalist

1967-1968
October 10   Lord Harlech (Sir David Ormsby-Gore), Member, House of Lords
December 5   Arthur C. Clarke, Author
February 27   A. E. Hotchner, Biographer
March 28[?]   Tom Poston, TV panelist, *To Tell the Truth*; Emmy

1968-1969
October 15   Meredith Wilson, Musician; Conductor
November 19   Bob Considine, Columnist; Author
January 21   Harrison Evans Salisbury, Asst. manag. ed., *New York Times*; Pulitzer Prize
March 4   Robert St. John, Correspondent

1969-1970
October 14   Betty Furness, Consumer advocate
December 2   Edward Weeks, Editor, *Atlantic Monthly*
January 27   Robert Pierpoint, Journalist
March 24   David Brinkley, TV correspondent

1970-1971
October 20   Ralph Nadar, Consumer advocate
November 10   Russell Baker, Satirist; Pulitzer Prize
January 19   Celeste Holm, Actress
February 2   Adm. Elmo Zumwalt, Jr., Chief of Naval Operations
March 23   Roger Hilsman, Former Asst. Secretary of State

1971-1972
October 19   Ray Bolger, Actor; Comedian
November 30   Alex Haley, Author; Pulitzer Prize
January 25   George Plimpton, Author
March 28   Roger Mudd, Correspondent, CBS

1972-1973
October 17   Max Lerner, Prof., American Civ. & World Politics, Brandeis University
December 5   Robert Novack & Ben Wattenberg, Columnists
January 30   Peter Maas, Author
March 6   Clare Booth Luce, Author; Congresswoman
April 3   Eugene Rostow, Educator; Economist

1973-1974
October 3   William F. Buckley, Columnist
February 5   Patrice Munsel, Opera star
March 12   Daniel Schorr, Correspondent
April 16   Judith Crist, Movie critic

1974-1975
October 15   Harry Reasoner, Correspondent, ABC
November 12   Dr. Daniel Boorstin, Dir., Nat. Museum of History & Technology; Rhodes Scholar; Pulitzer Prize
January 21   Samuel Dash, Former Chief Counsel, Senate Watergate Committee
February 18   Dr. Joyce Brothers, Columnist
March 24   Hugh Scott, Senator

1975-1976
October 28   John V. Lindsay, Former Mayor, New York City
December 2   Clark Kerr, Chair, Carnegie Council on Higher Education
January 13   Arthur M. Schlesinger, Jr., Historian; Pulitzer Prize
February 17   Rabbi Daniel J. Silver, Theologian; Author
March 30   Helen Thomas, Columnist

1976-1977
October 5   Hugh Sidey, Correspondent, *Time*
November 16   Daniel Patrick Moynihan, Senator
January 18   William J. Raspberry, Columnist, *Washington Post*; Pulitzer Prize
March 22   James J. Kilpatrick, Correspondent
May 3   Erma Bombeck, Author

1977-1978
October 4   Abba Eban, Former Israeli Foreign Minster
November 15   Peter Duchin, Composer; Pianist
January 10   Hedrick Smith, Journalist; Pulitzer Prize
February 21   Charles McDowell, Journalist; Humorist
April 27   Josh Logan, Playwright
May 24   Dr. Walter Heller, Author; Economist

1978-1979
November 21 | Nancy Dickerson, Correspondent; Author
January 27 | Ramsey Clark, Former U.S. Attorney General &
William Colby, Former director, CIA
February 20 | Mary Lee Settle, Author
March 20 | Bernard Kalb, Journalist
April 24 | Orson Bean, Actor

1979-1980
October 30 | Art Buchwald, Humorist
November 27 | William Sullivan, Diplomat
January 15 | Harry K. Smith, Former correspondent, ABC
April 22 | Reid Buckley & Nicholas Johnson
May 20 | Brendan Gill, Drama critic, *New Yorker*

1980-1981
October 21 | Charles Osgood, Correspondent
December 2 | B. Genry Lee, Dir., Jupiter Project
January 13 | Abigail Van Buren, Advice columnist
March 31 | Vincent Bugliosi, Former prosecutor
April 28 | William Proxmire, Senator

1981-1982
October 20 | Ray Brady, Journalist
December 1 | Sam Ervin, Former Senator
January 5 | Dr. Charles Jarvis, Humorist
February 23 | Coretta Scott King, Human rights activist
April 6 | Jack Anderson, Investigative reporter

1982-1983
October 12 | Robert Pierpoint, Correspondent, CBS
November 30 | George Gallup, Jr., Pres., Gallup Poll
January 25 | Drew Middleton, Military correspondent,
New York Times
March 8 | Mark Russell, Comedian
April 19 | Jody Powell, Former Press Secretary to Pres.
Jimmy Carter

1983-1984
November 1 | John O Marsh, Jr., Secretary of the Army
November 29 | Michael Annison, Futurist
January 17 | Anthony Lewis, Columnist, *New York Times*
March 6 | Jeff MacNelly, Political cartoonist;
3-time Pulitzer Prize
April 3 | Morris Abram, Former member,
U.S. Civil Rights Commission

1984-1985
November 24 | Anne Compton, Reporter, ABC
January 8 | Mortimer Adler, Educator
February 19 | William H. Webster, Director, FBI
February 28 | Charles Kuralt, Journalist
March 12 | Hayward Hale Brun

1985-1986
October 27 | Richard "Racehorse" Haynes, Attorney
November 19 | Charles McDowell, Journalist,
Richmond Times Dispatch
January 21 | Nicolas Von Hoffman, Columnist
February 11 | Larry King, Talk-show host, CNN
March 4 | Beverly Sills, Gen. Dir., New York City Opera

1986-1987
October 21 | Tom Wolfe, Author
November 11 | Bill Moyers, Former Press Secretary to
Lyndon B. Johnson; Journalist
February 16 | Carl Rowan, Former ambassador to Finland
March 23 | Jayne Meadows, Actress

1987-1988
October 20 | Pearl Bailey, Entertainer; Humanitarian
November 17 | Warren E. Burger, Former Chief Justice,
U.S. Supreme Court
February 15 | David Mccullough, Author; Pulitzer Prize
March 14 | Sander Vanocur, Moderator,
ABC's *Business World*

1988-1989
October 18 | H. Ross Perot, Businessman
November 22 | David Brinkley, Journalist
February 7 | Jane Brody, Health columnist, *New York Times*
March 14 | George F. Will, Columnist; Pulitzer Prize

1989-1990
September 20 | Gerald R. Ford, Former President
November 14 | Phyllis Schlafly, Conservative &
Sarah Weddington, Attorney; argued
Roe v. Wade
William B. Spong, Moderator
March 13 | Bobby Short, Musician
April 17 | Thomas P. O'Neill, Jr., Former Speaker
of the House

1990-1991
September 18 | Zbigniew Brzezinski, Former National Security
Advisor
October 9 | Ellen Goodman, Columnist; Pulitzer Prize
February 5 | Edward I. Koch, Former mayor, New York City
April 16 | Dr. C. Everett Koop, Former Surgeon General

1991-1992
September 30 | Dr. Henry A. Kissinger, Former Secretary of
State; Nobel Peace Prize
November 19 | Ann Landers, Advice columnist
February 11 | Clarence Page, Columnist; Pulitzer Prize
April 1 | Margaret Thatcher, Former Prime Minister,
Great Britain

1992-1993
September 29 | The Capitol Steps, Musical revue
November 17 | Robert Bork, Judge
January 24 | Tom Brokaw, Journalist, NBC

1993-1994
October 5 | Mario Cuomo, Former governor, New York
December 16 | Gene Siskel & Roger Ebert, Film critics
February 21 | George Bush, Former President, United States
April 12 | Peter V. Ueberroth, Olympic leader;
former Baseball Commissioner
May 4 | Dr. Jeane Kirkpatrick, Former ambassador
to U.N.

1994-1995

September 20	Colin Powell, Former Chair, Joint Chiefs of Staff
November 15	Robert MacNeil, Exec. Dir., News Hour
January 17	George Steinbrenner, Owner, New York Yankees
March 28	Mary Matalin & James Carville, Political advisors

1995-1996

September 19	Brian Mulroney, Former Canadian Prime Minister
November 7	Peter Lynch, Investment advisor
February 27	Ken Burns, Documentary film maker
March 26	Cokie Roberts, Journalist, ABC

1996-1997

September 17	Barbara Walters, Journalist, ABC
November 19	Mark Russell, Political satirist
February 11	Charlie Rose, James Fallows & Kevin Phillips, journalists
April 1	Jane Goodall, Animal researcher

1997-1998

October 15	John Major, Former Prime Minister, Great Britain
November 11	Robert Dole, Former senator
February 11	Ben Bradlee, Journalist
April 3	Dave Barry, Humorist

1998-1999 (scheduled)

October 1	Elizabeth Dole, Pres., American Red Cross
November 8	Dan Rather, Journalist
February 23	Gary Trudeau, Creator, *Doonesbury*
May 11	David Breshears, Producer, *Everest*

APPENDIX B
NORFOLK FORUM OFFICERS*

1932
President: Dr. Vincent H. Ober
Vice-President: Alfred Anderson
Secretary/Treasurer: Mrs. M. J. Caples

1933
President: J. E. Capps
1st Vice-President: E. S. Brinkley
2nd Vice-President: Mrs. Frederick R. Barrett
Corres. Secretary: Cherry Nottingham
Record. Secretary: Mrs. W. L. Harrell
Treasurer: Roy W. Dudley

1934
President: J. E. Capps
1st Vice-President: E. S. Brinkley
2nd Vice-President: Mrs. Frederick R. Barrett
Corres. Secretary: Cherry Nottingham
Record. Secretary: Mrs. W. L. Harrell
Treasurer: Roy W. Dudley
Ch., Program Comm.: Winder R. Harris

1935 (9 June)
President: J. E. Capps
Ch., Program Comm.: Winder R. Harris

1936
President: J. E. Capps
Ch., Program Comm.: Winder R. Harris

1937
President: J. E. Capps
Ch., Program Comm.: Winder R. Harris

1938 (June)
President: Winder R. Harris
1st Vice-President: Mrs. Frederick R. Barrett
2nd Vice-President: Michael B. Wagenheim
Secretary: Mrs. Kirk Montague
Treasurer: Samuel T. Northern
Ch., Program Comm.: Winder R. Harris
Ch., Program Comm.: Whit P. Tunstall (October)

1939 (July)
President: Winder R. Harris
1st Vice-President: Mrs. Frederick R. Barrett
2nd Vice-President: Michael B. Wagenheim
Secretary: Mrs. Kirk Montague
Treasurer: Samuel T. Northern
Ch., Program Comm.: Whit P. Tunstall

1940 (March)
President: Winder R. Harris
1st Vice-President: Mrs. Frederick R. Barrett
2nd Vice-President: Michael B. Wagenheim
Secretary: Mrs. Kirk Montague
Treasurer: Samuel T. Northern
Ch., Program Comm.: Whit P. Tunstall

1941 (February)
President: Winder R. Harris
1st Vice-President: Mrs. Fredrick R. Barrett
2nd Vice-President: Michael B. Wagenheim
Secretary: Cherry Nottingham
Treasurer: Samuel T. Northern
Ch., Program Comm.: Whit P. Tunstall

1941
President: Whit P. Tunstall
Honorary President: Winder R. Harris
1st Vice-President: Mrs. Frederick R. Barrett
2nd Vice-President: Michael B. Wagenheim
Secretary: Cherry Nottingham
Treasurer: Samuel T. Northern

1942
President: Whit P. Tunstall
Honorary President: Winder R. Harris
1st Vice-President: Mrs. Frederick R. Barrett
2nd Vice-President: Michael B. Wagenheim
Secretary: Cherry Nottingham
Treasurer: Samuel T. Northern
Ch., Program Comm.: Samuel T. Northern

* Based on records available.

1943
President: Lenoir Chambers
Honorary President: Winder R. Harris
1st Vice-President: Thomas H. Willcox
2nd Vice-President :   Mrs. A. O. Calcott
Secretary: Cherry Nottingham
Treasurer: Samuel T. Northern
Ch., Program Comm.:   W. McKenzie Jenkins

1944
President: Lenoir Chambers
1st Vice-President: Thomas H. Willcox
Secretary: Cherry Nottingham

1945
President: Lenoir Chambers
1st Vice-President: Thomas H. Willcox
2nd Vice-President: Charles T. Abeles
Secretary: Cherry Nottingham
Treasurer: Robert C. de Rosset

1946
President: Charles T. Abeles
1st Vice-President: Thomas H. Willcox
2nd Vice-President: Hugh B. G. Gault
Secretary: Cherry Nottingham
Treasurer: Robert C. de Rosset

1947
President: Charles T. Abeles
1st Vice-President: Thomas H. Willcox
2nd Vice-President: Mrs. Robert B. Tunstall
Secretary: Joseph A. Leslie, Jr.
Treasurer: Robert C. de Rosset
Ch., Board of Directors: Michael B. Wagenheim

1948 (June)
President: Charles T. Abeles
1st Vice-President: Thomas H. Willcox
2nd Vice-President: Joseph A. Leslie, Jr.
Secretary: Earnest P. Mangum
Treasurer: Robert C. de Rosset

1949
President: Charles T. Abeles
1st Vice-President: Joseph A. Leslie, Jr.
2nd Vice-President: Robert M. Hughes, Jr.
Secretary: Ernest P. Mangum
Treasurer: Robert C. de Rosset

1950
President: Joseph A. Leslie, Jr.
Honorary President: Charles T. Abeles
1st Vice-President: Robert M. Hughes, Jr.
2nd Vice-President: S. C. Lampert
Secretary: Ernest P. Mangum
Treasurer: Robert C. de Rosset

1951
President: Joseph A. Leslie, Jr.
Honorary President: Charles T. Abeles
1st Vice-President: Robert M. Hughes, Jr.
2nd Vice-President: S. C. Lampert
Secretary: Ernest P. Mangum
Treasurer: Robert C. de Rosset

1952
President: S. C. Lampert
1st Vice-President: Michael B. Wagenheim
2nd Vice-President: Cherry Nottingham
Secretary: Ernest P. Mangum
Treasurer: A. Vernon Sheffield

1953
President: S. C. Lampert
1st Vice-President: Michael B. Wagenheim
2nd Vice-President: Cherry Nottingham
Secretary: Ernest P. Mangum
Treasurer: A. Vernon Sheffield
Ch., Membership Comm.:   Lamar Davis

1954
President: Harold G. Sugg
1st Vice-President: Richard B. Spindle, III
2nd Vice-President: Cherry Nottingham
Secretary: Ernest P. Mangum
Treasurer: A. Vernon Sheffield

1955 (13 April)
President: Harold G. Sugg
Honorary Vice-Pres.:   Cherry Nottingham
1st Vice-President: Richard B. Spindle, III
2nd Vice-President: Vice Adm. R. O. Davis
Secretary: Ernest P. Mangum
Treasurer: A. Vernon Sheffield
Ch., Membership Comm.:   John F. Rixey, Jr.

1955 (24 September)
President: Harold G. Sugg
Honorary Vice-Pres.:   Cherry Nottingham
1st Vice-President: Richard B. Spindle, III
2nd Vice-President: Vice Adm. R.O. Davis
Secretary: John F. Rixey, Jr.
Treasurer: Stockton H. Tyler, Jr.
Ch., Membership Comm.:   Benjamin S. Burroughs

1956 (7 September)
President: Vice Adm. R. O. Davis
Honorary Vice-Pres.:   Cherry Nottingham
1st Vice-President: Richard B. Spindle, III
2nd Vice-President: Walter A. Page
Secretary: John F. Rixey, Jr.
Treasurer: Stockton H. Tyler, Jr.

1957 (19 April)
President: Vice Adm. R. O. Davis
Honorary Vice-Pres.: Cherry Nottingham
1st Vice-President: Richard B. Spindle, III
2nd Vice-President: Walter A. Page
Secretary: R. Cosby Moore
Treasurer: Stockton H. Tyler, Jr.

1958 (11 April)
President: Richard B. Spindle, III
Honorary Vice-Pres.: Cherry Nottingham
1st Vice-President: Walter A. Page
2nd Vice-President: Lewis W. Webb, Jr.
Secretary: R. Cosby Moore
Treasurer: Stockton H. Tyler, Jr.

1959
President: Richard B. Spindle, III
Honorary Vice-Pres.: Cherry Nottingham
1st Vice-President: Walter A. Page
2nd Vice-President: Lewis W. Webb, Jr.
Secretary: R. Cosby Moore
Treasurer: Stockton H. Tyler, Jr.
Ch., Membership Comm.: Benjamin S. Burroughs

1960
President: Walter A. Page
Honorary Vice-Pres.: Cherry Nottingham
1st Vice-President: Alan J. Hofheimer
2nd Vice-President: John F. Rixey, Jr.
Secretary: R. Cosby Moore
Treasurer: Stockton H. Tyler, Jr.

1961
President: Walter A. Page
Honorary Vice-Pres.: Cherry Nottingham
1st Vice-President: Alan J. Hofheimer
2nd Vice-President: John F. Rixey, Jr.
Secretary: Edward L. Ryan, Jr.
Treasurer: Stockton H. Tyler, Jr.

1962
President: Alan J. Hofheimer
Honorary Vice-Pres.: Cherry Nottingham
1st Vice-President: John F. Rixey, Jr.
2nd Vice-President: Edward L. Ryan, Jr.
Secretary: Richard F. Wood
Treasurer: Stockton H. Tyler, Jr.

1963
President: Alan J. Hofheimer
Honorary Vice-Pres.: Cherry Nottingham
1st Vice-President: John F. Rixey, Jr.
2nd Vice-President: Edward L. Ryan, Jr.
Secretary: Richard F. Wood
Treasurer: Stockton H. Tyler, Jr.

1964
President: John F. Rixey, Jr.
Honorary Vice-Pres.: Cherry Nottingham
Secretary: Richard F. Wood
Treasurer: Stockton H. Tyler, Jr.

1965
President: John F. Rixey
Honorary Vice-Pres.: Cherry Nottingham
1st Vice-President: Edward L. Ryan, Jr.
2nd Vice-President: C. Wiley Grandy, IV
Secretary: Richard F. Wood
Treasurer: Stockton H. Tyler, Jr.

1966
President: Edward L. Ryan, Jr.
1st Vice-President: G. William Whitehurst
2nd Vice-President: C. Wiley Grandy, IV
Secretary: Richard F. Wood
Treasurer: Stockton H. Tyler, Jr.

1967
President: Edward L. Ryan, Jr
1st Vice-President: G. William Whitehurst
2nd Vice-President: C. Wiley Grandy, IV
Secretary: Richard F. Wood
Treasurer: Stockton H. Tyler, Jr.

1968
President: G. William Whitehurst
1st Vice-President: William Beechman
2nd Vice-President: Glenn Scott
Secretary: Richard F. Wood
Treasurer: Stockton H. Tyler, Jr.

1968 (December)
President: Glenn Scott
1st Vice-President: William Beechman
Secretary: Richard F. Wood
Treasurer: Stockton H. Tyler, Jr.

1969
President: Glenn Scott
1st Vice-President: J. Hume Taylor, Jr.
2nd Vice-President: Morton H. Clark
Secretary: Richard F. Wood
Treasurer: Stockton H. Tyler, Jr.

1970
President: Glenn Scott
1st Vice-President: J. Hume Taylor, Jr.
2nd Vice-President: Morton H. Clark
Secretary: Richard F. Wood
Treasurer: Stockton H. Tyler, Jr.

1971

President:	J. Hume Taylor, Jr.
1st Vice-President:	Morton H. Clark
2nd Vice-President:	Dr. Lambuth M. Clarke
Secretary:	John M. Ryan
Treasurer:	Stockton H. Tyler, Jr.

1972

President:	J. Hume Taylor, Jr.
1st Vice-President:	Morton H. Clark
2nd Vice-President:	Dr. Lambuth M. Clarke
Secretary:	John M. Ryan
Treasurer:	Stockton H. Tyler, Jr.

1973

President:	J. Hume Taylor, Jr.
1st Vice-President:	Morton H. Clark
2nd Vice-President:	Dr. Lambuth M. Clarke
Secretary:	John M. Ryan
Treasurer:	Stockton H. Tyler, Jr.

1974

President:	Morton H. Clark
1st Vice-President:	John M. Ryan
2nd Vice-President:	Vincent J. Mastracco, Jr.
Secretary:	Betsy Trundle
Treasurer:	Stockton H. Tyler, Jr.

1975

President:	Morton H. Clark
1st Vice-President:	John M. Ryan
2nd Vice-President:	Vincent J. Mastracco, Jr.
Secretary:	Betsy Trundle
Treasurer:	Stockton H. Tyler, Jr.

1976

President:	John M. Ryan
1st Vice-President:	Vincent J. Mastracco, Jr.
2nd Vice-President:	Betsy Trundle
Treasurer:	Stockton H. Tyler, Jr.

1977 (September)

President:	Vincent J. Mastracco, Jr.
1st Vice-President:	Betsy Trundle
2nd Vice-President:	Dr. Willcox Ruffin, Jr.
Secretary:	Ashby W. Wilcox
Treasurer:	John W. Ballard, III

1978

President:	Vincent J. Mastracco, Jr.
1st Vice-President:	Betsy Trundle
2nd Vice-President:	Dr. Willcox Ruffin, Jr.
Secretary:	Ashby W. Willcox
Treasurer:	John W. Ballard, III
Ch., Program:	Betsy Trundle
Ch., Publicity and Membership:	Virginia Breeden
Ch., Arrangements:	Hunter W. Sims, Jr.
Ch., Entertainment:	Carter Grandy Scott

1979

President:	Vincent J. Mastracco, Jr.
1st Vice-President:	Betsy Trundle
2nd Vice-President:	Dr. Willcox Ruffin, Jr.
Secretary:	Ashby W. Willcox
Treasurer:	John W. Ballard, III

1980

President:	Betsy Trundle
1st Vice-President:	Dr. Willcox Ruffin, Jr.
2nd Vice-President:	Allan G. Donn
Secretary:	Mary Grandy
Treasurer:	Harvey W. Roberts
Ch., Program:	Dr. Willcox Ruffin, Jr.
Ch., Publicity and Membership:	Walter E. Hoffman, Jr.
Ch., Arrangements:	John Crumpler
Ch., Entertainment:	Mary Grandy

1981

President:	Dr. Willcox Ruffin, Jr.
1st Vice-President:	Allan G. Donn
2nd Vice-President:	Carter Grandy Scott
Secretary:	Walter E. Hoffman, Jr.
Treasurer:	Harvey W. Roberts, III

1982

President:	Dr. Willcox Ruffin, Jr.
1st Vice-President:	Allan G. Donn
2nd Vice-President:	Carter Grandy Scott
Secretary:	Walter E. Hoffman, Jr.
Treasurer:	Harvey W. Roberts, III

1983

President:	Allan G. Donn
1st Vice-President:	Walter E. Hoffman, Jr.
2nd Vice-President:	John Tucker, Jr.
Secretary:	Kathleen R. Steadman
Treasurer:	Harvey W. Roberts, III
Ticket Information:	Ann Branch
Ch., Ticket Sales:	Jim Matthews

1984

President:	Allan Donn
1st Vice-President:	Walter E. Hoffman, Jr.
2nd Vice-President:	John Tucker, Jr.
Secretary:	Kathleen R. Steadman
Treasurer:	Harvey W. Roberts, III
Ticket Information:	Ann Branch

1985

President:	Walter E. Hoffman, Jr.
1st Vice-President:	John Tucker, Jr.
2nd Vice-President:	Carter Grandy Scott
Secretary:	Kathleen R. Steadman
Treasurer:	Harvey W. Roberts, III
Ticket Information:	Ann Branch

1986

President:	Walter E. Hoffman, Jr.
1st Vice-President:	John H. Tucker, Jr.
2nd Vice-President:	Carter Grandy Scott
Secretary:	Kathleen R. Steadman
Treasurer:	Harvey W. Roberts, III
Ch., Program:	John H. Tucker, Jr.
Ch., Entertainment:	Jeannette Blount
Ch., Publicity:	Carter Grandy Scott
Ch., Membership:	Jeffrey A. Breit
Ch., Arrangements:	Lydia Taylor
Ch., Executive:	Walter E. Hoffman, Jr.
Ticket Information:	Mrs. William C. Eisenbeiss

1987

President:	John H. Tucker, Jr.
1st Vice-President:	Carter Grandy Scott
2nd Vice-President:	John P. Morison
Secretary:	Kathleen R. Steadman
Treasurer:	Thomas B. Shuttleworth
Ch., Program:	Carter Grandy Scott
Ch., Entertainment:	Jeannette Blount
Ch., Publicity:	William L. Nusbaum
Ch., Membership:	Gary N. Rubin
Ch., Arrangements:	Anne Shumadine
Ticket Information:	Mrs. William C. Eisenbeiss

1988

President:	John H. Tucker, Jr.
1st Vice-President:	Carter Grandy Scott
2nd Vice-President:	John P. Morison
Secretary:	Kathleen R. Steadman
Treasurer:	Thomas B. Shuttleworth
Ticket Information:	Mrs. William C. Eisenbeiss

1989

President:	Carter Grandy Scott
1st Vice-President:	John P. Morison
2nd Vice-President:	Monroe Kelly, III
Secretary:	Gerry Davis
Treasurer:	Thomas B. Suttleworth
Ch., Program:	John P. Morison
Ch., Entertainment:	Jeannette Blount
Ch., Publicity:	William L. Nusbaum
Ch., Membership:	Gary N. Rubin
Ch., Arrangements:	James S. Mathews
Ch., Executive:	Carter Grandy Scott

1990

President:	Carter Grandy Scott
1st Vice-President:	Monroe Kelly, III
2nd Vice-President:	James S. Mathews
Secretary:	Gerry Davis
Treasurer:	Thomas B. Shuttleworth
Ch., Program:	Monroe Kelly, III
Ch., Entertainment:	Jeannette Blount
Ch., Publicity & Management:	William L. Nusbaum
Ch., Arrangements:	John Matson
Ticket Information:	Lou Weaver

1991

President:	Monroe Kelly, III
1st Vice-President:	James S. Mathews
2nd Vice-President:	Thomas B. Shuttleworth
Secretary:	Jeannette Blount
Treasurer:	Gary N. Rubin
Ch., Program:	James S. Mathews
Ch., Entertainment:	Margo Taylor
Ch., Publicity:	William L. Nusbaum
Ch., Arrangements:	John Matson
Ticket Information:	Lou Weaver

1992

President:	Monroe Kelly, III
1st Vice-President:	Thomas B. Shuttleworth
2nd Vice-President:	Gary N. Rubin
Secretary:	Jeannette Blount
Treasurer:	Frederick V. Martin
Ch., Program:	Thomas B. Shuttleworth
Ch., Entertainment:	Margo Taylor
Ch., Publicity:	Kathryn Byler Clark
Ch., Arrangements:	William R. Van Buren, III
Ch., Long Range Planning:	Gary N. Rubin
Ticket Information:	Lou Weaver
Honorary Director:	Dr. Vincent H. Ober

1993

President:	Thomas B. Shuttleworth
1st Vice-President:	Jo Ann Hofheimer
2nd Vice-President:	William R. Van Buren, III
Secretary:	Jeannette Blount
Treasurer:	Frederick V. Martin
Ch., Program:	Jo Ann Hofheimer
Ch., Entertainment:	Catherine Train
Ch., Publicity:	Kathryn Byler Clark
Ch., Arrangements:	Everett Martin
Ch., Long Range Planning:	Carter Grandy Scott
Ticket Information:	Lou Weaver
Honorary Director:	Dr. Vincent H. Ober

1994

President:	Thomas B. Shuttleworth
1st Vice-President:	Jo Ann Hofheimer
2nd Vice-President:	William R. Van Buren, III
Secretary:	Jeannette Blount
Treasurer:	Frederick V. Martin
Ch., Program:	Jo Ann Hofheimer
Ch., Entertainment:	Kathleen Adams
Ch., Publicity:	Kathryn Byler Clark
Ch., Arrangements:	Everett Martin
Ch., Long Range Planning:	Arnold McKinnon
Ticket Information:	Lou Weaver
Honorary Director:	Dr. Vincent H. Ober

1995

President:	Jo Ann Hofheimer
1st Vice-President:	William R. Van Buren, III
2nd Vice-President:	Dr. L. D. Britt
Secretary:	Jeannette Blount
Treasurer:	Frederick V. Martin
Ch., Program:	Jo Ann Hofheimer
Ch., Entertainment:	Kathleen Adams
Ch., Publicity:	Kathryn Byler Clark
Ch., Arrangements:	William W. King
Ticket Information:	Lou Weaver

1996

President:	Jo Ann Hofheimer
1st Vice-President:	William R. Van Buren, III
2nd Vice-President:	Dr. L. D. Britt
Secretary:	Jeannette Blount
Treasurer:	Frederick V. Martin
Ticket Information:	Lou Weaver

1997

President:	William R. Van Buren, III
1st Vice-President:	Dr. L. D. Britt
2nd Vice-President:	William W. King
Secretary:	Alice Mountjoy
Treasurer:	Frederick V. Martin
Ch., Program:	William R. Van Buren, III
Ch., Entertainment:	Eleanor Harris
Ch., Publicity:	Alfred M. Randolph, Jr.
Ch., Arrangements:	Richard G. Diamonstein
Ticket Information:	Lou Weaver

1998

President:	William R. Van Buren, III
1st Vice-President:	Dr. L. D. Britt
2nd Vice-President:	William W. King
Secretary:	Alice Mountjoy
Treasurer:	Richard G. Diamonstein
Ch., Program:	Dr. L. D. Britt
Ch., Entertainment:	Eleanor Harris
Ch., Publicity:	Alfred M. Randolph, Jr.
Ch., Arrangements:	Wayne Wilbanks
Ticket Information:	Lou Weaver

Index

BC, 85
beles, Charles T., *31*, 33, 50, *50*, 51, 52
beles, Mrs., *50*
bend, Hallett, 36
dkins v. School Board of the City of Newport
    News, 54
frican American, 12, 13, *14*, 24, 68, 69, *83*
gar, Herbert, 35, 57
gnew, Spiro T., 54
lfaro, Ricardo, Dr., *40*, 41, *41*
ll-American City, 47, *47*
llen, Henry J., 38
lliance for Progress, 72
ltschul, Slyvan, Mrs., 46
mbassador to Denmark, *38*, 40
mbassador to Iran, 73
mbassador to South Vietnam, 72
merican Age, 38
merican Association of University Women,
    24
merican Mercury, 27, 45
nderson, Alfred, 18
ndrews, Mason C., 55, 63
nti-Semitism, 50
rgentine Diary, 39
rtists in Uniform, 38
sia, 25, 37, 38, 39, 40, 42, 56, 57, 72
tomic bomb, 45, 56, 57, 60, 61, 68, 71
ttlee, Clement R., *58*, 59, *59*, 76
ttorney general of the United States, 73
twater, Edith, 60
xis powers, 41
zalea Garden, 13, *14*

ailey, Pearl, 69
aker, Russell, 72
aldwin, Hanson, 70
anker's Trust Building, 25
arkley, Alben William, 30
arnard College, 24
arr, Stringfellow, 38, 40
arrett, Frederick, Mrs., 23, 25, 28
arron, Jim, 22
arry, Dave, *86*
ataan Island, 42
atten, Frank, *51*, *52*
eacon, 85
eckett v. School Board of the City of Norfolk, 54
ellah, James, 57
erg, Lewis, Dr., 30
erkley Machine and Iron Works, 50
erlin Conference, *59*
ig Tree Club, 28
kini Atoll, 57
inford, P. N., 27
rth control, 38
lair Auditorium, 9, 29, 30, 30, *30*, 31, 41
lair Junior High School, 9, *26*, 28, 31, 37
lount, Jeannette, 53
oard term limits, 51
ogger, Tommy, 15, 45
olger, Ray, 72

Boorstin, Daniel J., 89
Bork, Robert, *75*
Boston Transcript, 55
Boyle and Priest, 50
Boys' Club of Norfolk, 19
Bradley, David, Dr., 57
Brandies University, 63
Breeden Jr., Edward L., 54
Breshears, David, *88*
Brinkley, Edward Stanley, 28
British ambassador, 72
British consulate, 60
British Prime Minister, 56, 59, *59*, *74*, 76, *80*,
    82, *83*
Britt, L. D., Dr., 83, *83*, 89
Brokaw, Tom, 87
Brown v. Board of Education, 52
Brundage, W. Fitzhugh, 20
Bryan, John Steward, 24
Bryan, William Jennings, 40
Brzezinski, Zbigniew, 76
Buchwald, Art, 72
Burger, Warren E., 76
Burns, Ken, 85
Burroughs, Benjamin S., 48, 55
bus service, 69
Bush, George, 76, 77, *79*
Business and Professional Woman's Club, 55
Byrd, Harry Flood, 20, 21, 22, 54

C

Cable News Network, 85
Cadman, S. Parkes, Dr., 41, 42
Calcott, A. O., Mrs., 46, 47, 49, 52, 55, 56,
    84
Canadian Prime Minister, 76, *81*, 82
Capitol Steps, *76*
Caples, M. J., Mrs., 18
Capps, J. E., 25, 28, *28*, 29, *31*, 51, 75
Carter, James E. "Jimmy", *67*, *67*, 76
Cavalier Beach Club, 50
census, 12
Center Theater, 31, *48*, 49, 52, *62*, 63, 64, 65
Central Conference of American Rabbis
    Yearbook, 22
Central Congregational Church, 41
Central Intelligence Agency, 73
Central Powers, 50
Chamber of Commerce, 51
Chamberlin Hotel, 21, 22
Chambers, Lenoir, 7, *20*, 27, 28, 32, 34, 35,
    35, 36, 37, 39, 46, 47, 48, 49, 50, 51,
    51, 54, 60, 67
Chattanooga News, 30
Chesapeake Bay Bridge-Tunnel, 63
Chief of Naval Operations, 66, *66*
Children's Home Society of Virginia, 19
Childs, Marquis W., *67*, 68, 70
Childs-Redfield, Malissa, 67, 68
China, 9, 38, 40, 61
Christian Science Monitor, 42
Christian, 21, 23
Chrysler Hall, 49, *64*, 75, 77, 83
Chrysler Jr., Walter P., 63

Chrysler Museum, *12*, 63
Chrysler, Jean Outland, 63
Churchill, Winston, 57, 59, 75
City Auditorium, 29, 30
City Hall Avenue, *10*, *46*
Civil War, 17, 64
Civil Works Administration, *14*
civil rights, 45, 64
Clark, Morton H., 68
Clark, Ramsey, 73
Clay, Henry, 17
Close, Upton, 37
closed-circuit television, 83
Colby, William, 73
Cold War, 45, 56, 57, 59, 61, 64, 77
College of William and Mary, 24, 28, 32, 53,
    54
Collier's, 27
Colonial Theater, 29
Columbia Broadcasting System (CBS), 70, 71
Columbia University, 22, 24, 28, 35
Commager, Henry Steele, 17
Commander in Chief, U.S. Atlantic Fleet, 66
Committee of One Hundred, 55
Committee on Public Information, 35
Communism, 37, 38, 39, 59, 66, 71
Communist Eleven, 58
Communist Party, 58
Community Home Achievement Award, 47
competition, 84, 85
Congress Party, 60
Congress, 22, 23, 33, 51, 65
Constitution Bicentennial Commission, 76
Contemporary Verse, 55
Cosmopolitan Club of Norfolk, 33, 56
Council of Europe, 59
Cox, James M., 32
Creel, George, 35
Crestar Bank, 50
Cuba, 71, 72
Cuban Missile Crisis, 57, 70
Cutchins, Clifford, 80

D

d'Art Center, 69
Dalton, Ted, 54
Darden Jr., Colgate W., *22*, 22, 23, 33, 56, 65
Dash, Samuel, 73
Davidson College, 53
Davis, R. O., Vice Admiral, 55, *65*, 66
de la Guardia, Ricardo Adolfo, 41
de Rosset, Robert C., 50
Dean, Vera Micheles, 18
debate format, 39, 40
Defur Hospital, 18
Dekker, Albert, 60
Democracy, 39
Denfeld, Louis E., Admiral, 66, *66*
Denmark, 41
Depression and the New Deal in Virginia, 12
Depression, The, 9, 11, 12, 13, 15, 25, 27, 36
Dern, George, 21
Diamonstein, Richard G., *86*, *89*
dinner attire, 36, 40

District of Columbia, *75*
Dole, Elizabeth, 78, *88*
Dole, Robert, 78, 86
Donn, Allan, 65, 79
Dozier, Turner, 51
Duchin, Peter, 72
Duckworth, Fred W., 54
Dudley, Roy W., 28, *28*
Dudley, Roy, Mrs., *28*
Duke University, 19
Dumar, Robert G., *75*
Durant, Will, Dr., 32, 38
Durham Sun, 19

E

Eastern Virginia Medical School, 63
Eastman, Max Forrester, 37
Eban, Abba, 73
Eisenhower, Dwight D., 54, 68, 86
Emonds, Richard H., 17
endowment fund, 80, 81
Enters, Agna, 60
Ervin, Sam, 73
Europe, 38, 56
Ewell, Tom, 72
Executive Club, 32

F

Fascism, 39, 42
Federal Bureau of Investigation, 57, 58, 73
Federal District Court judge, 53
Feldman Chamber Music Society, 46
Feldman, I. E., 46
Feldshuh, Tovah, 84
Fifth Naval District, 66
First Citizen Award, *28*
Fish Jr., Hamilton, *31*, 38, 39, 75
Fitzgerald, F. Scott, 85
Ford Motor Company, 15
Ford, Gerald R., *78*, 76
Foreign Policy Association (FPA), *16*, 18, 66
foreign affairs, 76
Foreman Field, *12*, 13
Fraim, Paul, *83*
France, 39, 42
Freemason Street Baptist Church, 22
Friddell, Guy, *52*, 54, 85
Furness, Betty, 69

G

Gandhi, Mahatma K., 60, 61
gas rationing, *36*, 36
Gatson, Paul M., 17
German Club, 35
Germany, 39, 42
Glass, Carter, 21
Goette, John, 27, 42
Goodall, Jane, *82*, 86
Goodman, Augusta S., 50
Gordon, C. M., Reverend, 31, 84
Governor of Virginia, 23
Granby Street, *36*
Grandy IV, C. (Cyrus) Wiley, 55, 59

Grandy, Ann, 59
Gray, Ernest W., Dr., 31, 32
Great Adventure Lecture Series, 19, 84
Great Britain, 39, 59, 60, 75
Greensboro Daily News, 35
Gresham, E. T., *32*
Guantanamo Bay, 72
Guerry, William Moultrie, 53
Guthrie, James, 60

H
Haiti, 67, *67*
Haley, Alexander "Alex" Palmer Murray, 69
Hamilton, Cosmo, 30
Hamilton, Norman R., 22, 33, 65
Hampton Roads Bridge Tunnel, 63
Hampton Roads, 9, 11, 13, 69, *75*, 89
Hardy Jr., Porter,
Harrell, W. L., Mrs., 28
Harris, Winder R., 21, 28, *32*, 32, 45, 51, *52*, 65
Harrison Opera House, *48*
Harsch, Joseph C., 42
Harvard University, 50, *50*, 57, 72
Haynesworth, Hugh C., Rear Admiral, 66
heads of state, 41, 56, 76
Hebrew Union College, 21
Heinemann, Ronald L., 12
High Spots of the Week's News, 33
Hill, Max, 36
Hilsman, Roger, 72, 73
Hindus, Maurice, 43
Hoffman, Walter E., 53, 54, 55
Hofheimer II, Henry Clay, 55
Hofheimer, Alan J., *33*
Hofheimer, Jo Ann, 79, *82*
Holm, Celeste, 72
House Armed Services Committee, 65
House of Delegates, 22
Hudson, J. Carlton, *31*
Hutchens, Robert E., Dr., 21

I
I Led Three Lives, 58
incorporation, 33, 36
India, 59, 60, 61
Indian ambassador to the United States, 60
Internal Revenue Service, 80
Israeli Foreign Minister, 73
Italy, 42
Izac Committee, 45
Izac, Edouard V. M., 45

J
Jaffé, Alice, 23, 46
Jaffé, Louis I., 7, 19, 20, *20*, 21, 23, 24, 35, 52, *52*, 53
Japan, 37, 38, 39
Jewish, 21, 22, 23
Johnson, Lyndon B., 69, 73
Johnson, Thomas M., 53
Joint Chiefs of Staff, 67
Josephs, Ray, 39
Junior League of Norfolk and Virginia Beach, 84
Justice, Gene, 64

K
Kai-shek, Chiang, 40
Kaltenborn, H. V., *30*
Kanter, Harry, *33*
Katsias, Kathy, 85
Kaufman, Charles, *32*, *33*
Kelly III, Monroe, *74*, *76*, *85*
Kelly, Walter Crawford, 59, 60, *61*
Kennedy, John F., 71, 72
Kill and Overkill, 71
King, Coretta Scott, 69
King, Larry, 85
King, William W. "Will", *89*
Kissinger, Henry A., Dr., 72, 76, *77*
Kitchin, Lee, 81
Kiwanis Club of Norfolk, 19
Knickerbocker, H. H., 42, 43
Kunta Kinte, 69

L
La Follete Jr., Robert M., *31*, 32, 38, 39, 75
La Follette, Philip, 75
Labour Party, 59
Lafeber, Walter, 38
Landmark Communications, 53
Lapp, Ralph E., Dr., 57, 71, 72
Larchmont Methodist Church, 17
Larson, Arthur, Dr., 71
Latin America, 39, 41, 72
Laughton, A. W., Mr., 48, 49
Lazaron, Mike, *33*
Leache Memorial, Irene, 32
Leafe, Joseph, *84*
Ledger-Dispatch, 7, 31, 35, 48, 50, 52
Ledger-Star, 7, 51
Leidholdt, Alexander S., 20, 29, 34
Lerner, Max, 63
Leslie Jr., Joseph A., 49, 52, *52*
Leuchtenburg, William E., 17
Ley, Willy, 71
Leyte Gulf, *42*
Lindsay, John V., 73
Linkhorn Park School, 69
Lippman, Walter, 20, 21
Little Theater, 63
Lodge, Henry Cabot, 72
Longworth, Alice Roosevelt, 75
Look, 47
Louisville Courier-Journal, 35, 57
Lynching in the New South, 20
lynchings, 20
Lyric, 55

M
MacArthur, Douglas, General 42, *42*
Madrid, Amulfo Arias, 41
Madrid, Harmodia Aria, 41
Major, John, 76, 78, 82, *83*
Manchuria, 40
Manhattan Project, 57
Mann, Erika, 75
Mann, Thomas, 75
Mansbach, Harry, *33*
Manufacturers' Record, 1889, 17
Margulis, Ralph, *33*
Marriott Hotel, 83
Marsh Jr., John O., 73
Marshall Plan, 57
Marshall, George, 57

Martin Jr., Everett, 53, *75*
Martin Jr., Roy B., 54, *54*, 55, 63, 82, 83, 84
Martin, Frederick, 80
Marx, Karl, 57
Mason, Robert, *51*
Mason, Vivian Carter, 45
Massenberg Act, 24
Massenberg, George Alvin, 24
Masses, The, 37
Massive Resistance, 52, 53, 54
Matson, John P., *77*
Matson, Marianne, *77*
Matthews, Jim, 65
Maury High School, 24
Mayor of New York City, 73
McClaskey, Mark A., 27
McCullough, David, 80
McDine, Lucretia Libby, 11
McKinnon, Arnold, *67*
McKinnon, Oriana, *67*
Meacham, William S., 20, *52*
Medical Center Hospital, 50
Medical Tower, 63
Medina, Harold R., 49, 58
membership, 25, 28, 29, 30, *40*, 46, 47, 48, 49, 52, 63, 64, 65, 68, 75, 76, 78, 79, 80, 82, 83, 85
Mendoza, Louis D., Dr., 21, *21*, 22, 31, *33*, 84
Metropolitan Bank and Trust, 13
Middleton, Ray, 72
Miller, Paul David, Admiral, 66
Milton, George Fort, 30
Minakuchi, Yutaka, Dr., 40
Mitchell, Thomas, 72
Monroe, James, 17
Montague, Martha R., 37
Monticello Hotel, 16, 87
Monynihan, Daniel Patrick, 73
Morris, Richard Brandon, 17
Moslem League, 60
Mountjoy, Alice, *89*
Muggeridge, Malcolm, 72
Mulroney, Brian, 76, *81*, 82
Municipal Auditorium, 30
Municipal Park, *14*
Munsel, Patrice, 72
Museum of Natural History, 60

N
Nash, Ogden, 60
Nash, William Herbert, 37
National Association for the Advancement of Colored People, 54
National Bank of Commerce, *10*, 33
National Security Advisor, 76
Naval Base, 27
Naval Supply Center, 66
Naziism, 41
NBC, 87
Nehru, Jawaharlal, 61
New Deal, *12*, 12, 13, 17, 37, 38
New Norfolk, 51
New South, 17, 35
New South Creed, The, 17
New York Herald Tribune, 20
New York Times, 84
Newby, L. L., Mrs., 23
Newsweek, 47
Nixon, Richard M., 71, 76

No Place to Hide, 57
Nobel Peace Prize, 11, 70, 76, *77*
Norfolk, 11, 13, 15, 27, *44*, 47, *47*, 63
Norfolk Academy, 48
Norfolk Advertising Board, 22
Norfolk Anti-Tuberculosis League, 56
Norfolk Area Medical Center Authority, 63
Norfolk Arts Festival, 63
Norfolk Botanical Garden, 13, *14*
Norfolk Business and Professional Woman's Club, 24
Norfolk City Federation of Home and School League, 56
Norfolk Commission on Higher Education, 51
Norfolk Community Fund, 33
Norfolk Community Hospital, 13
Norfolk Council Committee on Higher Education, 20
Norfolk Division of the College of William and Mary, 24, 32, 54
Norfolk Forum (origins of), 11, 37
Norfolk Foundation, 51, 80, 81
Norfolk General Hospital, 20, 63
Norfolk Kiwanis Club, 84
Norfolk Landmark, 24
Norfolk Museum of Arts and Sciences, *12*, 13, 51, 63
Norfolk Naval Shipyard, *15*
Norfolk Newspaper Building, *34*
Norfolk Newspapers, Inc., 20
Norfolk School Board, 18, 29, 56
Norfolk Scope, *54*, 77, 82, 83
Norfolk State University, 68
Norfolk Town Meetings, 31, 84
Norfolk War Finance Committee, 50
Norfolk Yacht and Country Club, 35
Norfolk-Portsmouth Forum of Public Affairs, 11, 18, 23
Norfolk: The First Four Centuries, 15, 45
North Atlantic Treaty Organization (NATO), 46, 59, 77
Northern, Samuel T., *32*, 34, 55
Nottingham, Cherry, 23, 24, 28, 31, 33, 37, 50, 55, 84, 86
Nottingham, S. Severn, 24
Nuclear Science Service, 57
nuclear energy, 57
Nunn, Ira, 66
Nunn, Sam, 67

O
O'Neill Jr., Thomas P. "Tip", 76, *76*
Ober, Merrill J., 17
Ober, Vincent H., Dr., 11, 15, 17, 18, *18*, 19, *19*, 33, 66, 84, 86, 87
Oberndorfer, William, *33*
Office of Defense Health and Welfare Services, 27
Office of Price Administration, 36
Office of Strategic Services (OSS), 59
Ohef Sholom Temple, 21, 22, *33*
Old Dominion University, 13, 24, 32, 54, 80, 83, 84
Old Point Comfort, 21
Operation Crossroads, 57
Ormsby-Gore, David (Lord Harlech), Sir, 72
Outstanding Woman Award, 56
Owen, Ruth Bryan, 32, *38*, 40, 41
Oxford University, 22, 40

P

Pacific Mutual Life Insurance Company, 28
Page, Clarence, 68, 69
Page, Walter, 53
Palmes Academiques, 24
Pan-America, 30, 38
Panama, 41, *41*
Pandit, Vijaya, Madam, 61
Parade, 89
Parent-Teacher Association, 56
Park, No-yung, Dr., 40
Parramore, Thomas C., 15, 45
Patrick Henry School, *14*
Patterson, Donald, 53
Pavilion, 85
Pearl Harbor, *40*
Perot, Ross, *77*
Philadelphia College of Osteopathy, 17
Philadelphia Osteopathic Hospital, 18
Philbrick, Herbert, 57, 58
Philippines, 42
Pierpoint, Robert, 70
Pilot, 20, 21, 22, 25, 29, 30, 31, 40, 47, 49, *52*, 54, 55, 59, 68, 69, 72
Pogo, 59, *61*
Port Folio, 69
Portsmouth Forum, 32, 56, 84
Portsmouth, 48, 49
Poston, Tom, 72
Powell, Colin, *67*, 69
Powell, Jody, 73
Prentis Park (Portsmouth), 17
President's Lecture Series, 80, 84
Presidential Press Secretary, 73
Presidents Day, 77
Price, Vincent, 72
Pride and Prejudice: School Desegregation and Urban Renewal in Norfolk, 1950–1959, 54
Priest, Jennifer Gregory, 22
Princess Anne High School, 69
Progressive Party, 32
Proxmire, William, 73
Public Works Administration, 29
Pulitzer Prize, 11, 20, 38, 42, *51*, 53, 57, 69, *71*, 80

Q

question-and-answer period, 39, 42, *74*

R

Race Relations, 45, 52, 54, 55, 68
Rainey, Henry T., 25, 37, *37*
Raleigh Times, 32
Raman, T. A., 60
Raspberry, William J., 68, 69
Rather, Dan, *88*
Rau, Benegal, Sir, 60
Rau, Rama, Lady, 60, 61
Reagan, Ronald, 63
Reasoner, Harry, 71
Red Cross News Service, 19
Republican Looks at His Party, A, 71
Rhodes Scholar, 38, 40
Richardson, Elliott, 54
Rio de Janeiro conference, 41
Roberts, Cokie, 85
Romulo, Carlos, 42, *42*
Roosevelt, Franklin D., *12*, 22, 27, 37, 38

Roosevelt, Theodore, 75
Roots, 69
Rose, Charlie, 78
Rosenthal, A. M., 84
Rotary Club of Norfolk, 19, 32, 33
Rowan, Carl, 68, 69
Rubin, Gary, 80
Ruehlmann, William, 11, 79, 80
Ruffin Jr., Willcox, Dr., 65, *78*
Ruffin, Anne, *78*
Ruml, Beardsley, 36
Russell, Mark, 72, 78
Russia, 42

S

Sabbath School Extension of the Union of American Hebrew Congregations, 21
Salisbury, Harrison, 70, *71*
Saltonstall, Leverett, *50*
Saltwater & Printer's Ink, 32, *35*
Sanford, Jennifer, 53
Saturday Evening Post, 45
Savage, T. D., *40*
Schenck, Charles H., 46, 47
Schenkman, Edgar, 46
Schorr, Daniel, 70
Schwarz, Jacob, 22
Scott, Carter Grandy, 18, 59, 60, *61*, *76*, *77*, 80, *84*, 84
Scott, Glenn, *52*, 65, 67, 70, *77*, 80
Scott, Hugh, 73
Scott, Robert L., Brigadier General, 66
Seaboard Airline Railway, 50
Seaboard Citizens National Bank, 50, 51
Second Congressional District, 22, *32*, 33, 54, 65
Secret Missions: The Story of an Intelligence Officer, 59, 66
Secretary of State, 76
Secretary of the Army, 73
Secretary of the Navy, 21
Secretary of War, 21
segregation, 24, 54, 55
Senate Internal Security Subcommittee, 58
Seventy-fourth Congress, 22
Seventy-third Congress, 22
Shadrick, Thomas S., 53
Shafer World Peace Lecture, W. B., 81
Shafer World Peace Trust, W. B., 81, 82, *82*, 83
Shafer, Bruce, 81
Sheean, Vincent, 43, 56
Sherrick, Lester, *33*
Short, Bobby, 69
Shuttleworth, Marian, *67*, *79*, 85
Shuttleworth, Thomas, *67*, 81
Smith Academy, 50
Smith and Welton, 24, 29
Smith, Nicol, 59
Smith, Oscar, *28*
Smith, Oscar, Mrs., *28*
Smith, Rebecca Beach, 53
socialism, 37
Sorbonne, 24
South, 17, 35
Southern History Collection at the University of North Carolina, 35
Soviet Union, 38, 56, 66, 70, 71, 72, 77, 78
Speaker of the House, 25, 76
speaker fees, 43, 80

speaker variety, 72, 76, 78
Spindle III, Richard B., 53, 55
St. John's College, 40
Stalin, Josef, *59*
Standing Before the Shouting Mob, 19, 34
State Highway Commission, 22
State School Trustees Association, 56
state attorney general, 54
Steadman, Kathy, 76
Stecker Jr., John F., Dr., *85*
Stewart, Peter, 15, 45
Stickney, H. O., Rear Admiral, 66
Stone, William T., *16*, 18, 66
Suffolk, 40
Sugg, Harold G., 48, 52, *52*, 53, 60
Sullivan, William, 73
Supreme Allied Command, Atlantic, 46
Supreme Court justice, 76
surveys, 75, 78, 83
Swanson, Claude A., 21
Sweet Briar College, 69

T

Taylor Jr., J. Hume, 64, 68
Taylor, Gordon, 81
Taylor, Lydia Calvert, 53, *75*, 81
Temple University, 17
Thatcher, Margaret, *74*, 77, *80*, 82
Thompson, Dorothy, 75
Thompson, Thomas P., 29
Thornton, Daniel, *32*
ticket prices, 25, 79, 80
tickets, 11, 28, 29, 49, 52, 64, 65, 77, 83, 85
Tidewater Jewish Forum, 84
Tidewater, 55
Time, 56
Trinity College, 19
Trudeau, Gary, *88*
Truman, Harry S., 30, 56, *59*
Trundle, Betsy, 69
Tucker Jr., John H., *82*
Tunstall, Virginia Lynn, 55
Tunstall, Whit P., 33, 34
Turin, Francis E., 22
Tyler Jr., Stockton H., 50, 51

U

U.S. District Court of Appeals, *75*
U.S. House of Representatives, 9, 22
United Nations, 23, 42
United Service Organization (USO), 30, 31
United States Air Force, 66
United States Army, 35, 57
United States Foreign Service, 40
United States Information Agency, 71
United States Marine Corps, 22
United States Navy, 13, 50, 65, *65*, 66
Universal News Service, 32
University of Chicago, 24, 40
University of Cincinnati, 21
University of Madrid, 24
University of North Carolina, 35
University of Pennsylvania, 17, 53
University of Virginia, 17, 22, 23, 40, 54, 56
Untermeyer, Louis, 60
Uris, Leon, 84
USO Auditorium, 42
USS *Rowan*, *15*
USS *Stack*, *15*

V

Van Buren III, William R., *83*, 88, 89
Vietnam, 64, 72, 73
Virginia Beach Forum, 83, 84, 85
Virginia Club, 35
Virginia Commission on Interracial Cooperation, 20
Virginia Federation of Woman's Clubs, 23
Virginia Osteopathic Association, 19
Virginia Public Assemblage Act of 1926, 24
Virginian-Pilot, 7, 11, 12, 19, 22, 31, 32, *32*, 33, *34*, 35, 36, 45, *51*, 52, 53, 60, 65, 66, 67, 71, 77, 79, 84, 85
Von Trapp, Baroness, 72

W

W. Colston Leigh, Inc., 46
Wagenheim, Michael, *33*, 36, 55
Wallace, Henry A., 67
Walters, Barbara, 78
War Loan Campaigns, 50
war on drugs, 76
Ward, James H., Rear Admiral, 66
Warner, John, *79*
Washington and Lee University, 53
Washington Park, 9
Washington Post, 69
Watergate, 71, 73
Waterside Drive, 51
Webster, William H., 73
Weeks, Edward A., 36
Wells Theater, 83
Wendt, Gerald, Dr., 56, 57
White Sail Set, A, 55
White, Forrest P., 54
Whitehurst, G. William, Dr., *9*, 65, 67, 76
WHRO, 83
Willcox, Savage, Dickson, Hillis, and Ely, P.C., 65
Willcox, Thomas H., 55
William and Mary Stadium, *12*
Wilson, Meredith, 72
Wolfe, Henry C., 40
Woman of Achievement, 24
Woman's Club of Norfolk, 23
Woman's Council For Interracial Cooperation (WCIC), 23, 45, 56
Women Leaders, 23, 55
Wood, Joseph, *30*
Woodberry Forest School, 34, 35
Woodrow Wilson High School, 49
Works Project Administration, *14*
World Affairs Council of Hampton Roads, 19
World War I, 35, 37
World War II, 45, *48*, 56, 59, 60
WTAR (radio station), *19*

Y

Young Women's Christian Association, 23

Z

Z-grams, 66
Zacharias, E. M., Rear Admiral, 31, 59, 66
Zumwalt Jr., Elmo R., Admiral, 66, *66*

About the Author

Paul Chandler Moulton was born in Lucasville, Ohio, in 1959, and moved to Richmond, Virginia, with his family in 1970. After graduating from high school he joined the United States Navy, in his words, to "see the world and get a peacoat." Following his twelve-and-a-half years in the Navy, he enrolled at Old Dominion University and graduated in 1995 cum laude with a B.A. in history. Mr. Moulton has presented scholarly papers at the Graduate Conference on Southern History, Center for the Study of Southern Culture, University of Mississippi; Friends of Women's Studies Conference on Feminist Scholarship in Hampton Roads, Old Dominion University; Southwestern Social Science Association Conference, New Orleans, Louisiana; and the Virginia Humanities Conference, Mary Washington College, Fredericksburg, Virginia. His published work includes interviews with historians Dr. William E. Leuchtenburg and Dr. Wilson D. Miscamble in the *Old Dominion Historical Review*; "African-American Inclusion in the Fifth Naval District, 1942-1944," which appeared in the spring 1997 edition of the *Southern Historian*; and six articles for the *Encyclopedia of Civil Rights in America*. He is a member of Phi Alpha Theta, Virginia Historical Society, and the Southern Historical Society.